Dark Tales of
Old Cheshire

Angela Conway

Published by Sigma Leisure - an imprint of
Sigma Press, 1 South Oak Lane, Wilmslow, Cheshire SK9 6AR, England.

British Library Cataloguing in Publication Data
A CIP record for this book is available from the British Library.

ISBN: 1-85058-419-2

Typesetting and Design by: Sigma Press, Wilmslow, Cheshire.

Cover design and illustrations: Martin Mills

Photographs: The photograph on page 35 was kindly supplied by Capesrhorne Hall; all others were provided by the author.

Printed by: J.W. Arrowsmith Ltd, Bristol.

Acknowledgements: Thankyou to Karen "Cuddly Kaz" Cliff, for her invaluable help with the research; Martin Mills for the illustrations and support; my parents, Jim and Mary, and sister Jane, also for their support; and Bagpus, Byron and Ozzy for keeping me laughing! Thanks also to Vivienne Rae-Ellis and Muriel Armand for their kind permission and letters.

Dedication: To Martin Connor, for all your help with the manuscript, but most of all for just being there when I need you.

Preface

Surprisingly, it has been rather hard to find a wealth of information on Cheshire's darker and more mysterious events. However, that is not so with the ghost stories, as Cheshire has many historic and stately homes, of which nearly all claim some supernatural association. Some of the ghost stories included are traditional, but many others are modern accounts, and continuing as I write.

The folklore section shows us all a completely different way of life – one that we must not criticise, but praise for the Cheshire folks' ingenuity in times when there were no such things as hospitals, pills, immunisation and good sanitation. The very revival of herbal remedies and alternative medicines is a recognition that, although many of their methods are strange to us, they did get some of it right!

A point to bear in mind also, is that many tales which seem fantastic and hard to believe, have probably fallen victim to the "colouring" of time – meaning that an account, once factual, has been expanded and exaggerated with the passage of time. This is especially true in the case of folklore where nearly all stories were told by word of mouth, allowing personal prejudices, and the desire to be an interesting story-teller, take precedence over the accuracy of facts.

By taking "old Cheshire" as my area of reference, I include areas such as the Wirral which no longer form part of the county. I hope to show you that Cheshire was once much larger, and more respected, whereas today it seems to have lost much of its individual identity.

Hopefully, this book will show residents and non-residents alike that Cheshire has a fascinating history, always pervaded by the belief in forces unknown.

Angela Conway

Contents

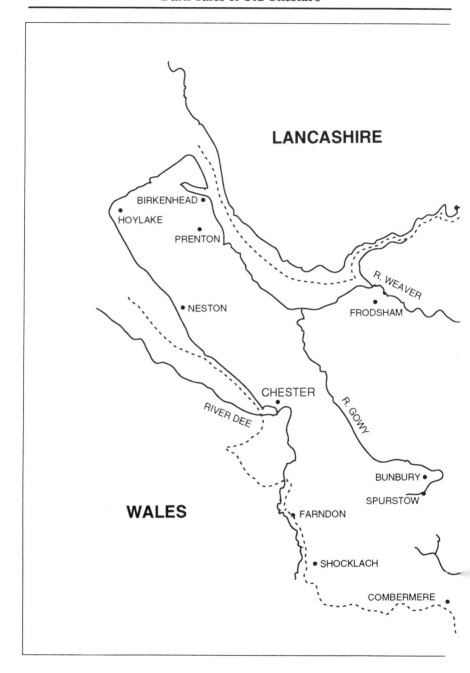

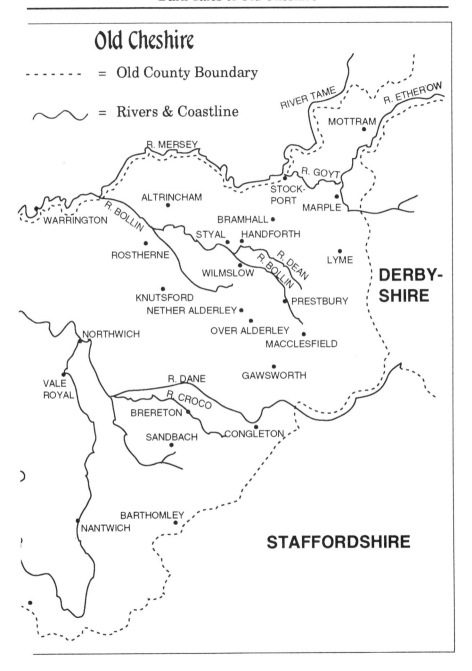

ix

1

Cheshire Ghosts

The Mysteries of Mauldeth

Mauldeth Hall in Stockport, better known as Mauldeth Home, was built around 1830 by a Mr. Dyer, and originally named Leegate. In 1854 it was bought by the Ecclesiastical Commissioners for the first and second Bishops of Manchester. The first died shortly after moving in, and the second found the Hall unbearable and thought of it "with dread". It was again sold in 1871 to a William Calendar, who died just five years later. It then passed to the "Northern Counties Hospital for Incurables", and was extended before the first patients were admitted in 1882. For over one hundred years it treated disabled and terminally ill patients, and was described as having "a real family atmosphere".

However, in April 1978, the Stockport Express carried a shocking story about the Home. Three priests of different denominations were called in to perform what is now called a "displacement service", to quieten some supposed supernatural activity.

The Stockport Area Health Authority had decided to take such drastic action, after many nurses at the Home threatened to resign, or ask for transfers. One nurse said "This is a spooky place at the best of times, but now everybody is terrified. The ghost has been seen on one of the corridors and reminds people of a patient who died a few months ago". Nurses also said they had been touched, and even scratched by the ghost, which was apparently so clear that they could make out every detail of her face and body. Many thought it was an old woman, who had been a patient there until she died three months before the priests were called in. There had been some tales of weird goings-on at the Home before (one source has said that an exorcism had been carried out there in the 1960s), but by April 1978 it had escalated to nightly visitations from the phantom!

As a consequence, a service was performed, in the middle of the night, by a Roman Catholic priest, an Anglican canon, and a Non-Conformist minister. They were Father Patrick Kavanagh of St Winifred's in Heaton Mersey, Canon Edwin Taylor of St Paul's Church and the Reverend Peter Killick of Heaton Moor United Reformed Church. Rev. Killick later said "There had been cases of an appearance in a particular place. We read a short service and said prayers in the hope that this would do the trick".

During the service, four people claimed to have seen the apparition of the old woman, although the staff were keeping very quiet about it the following day, and not revealing much information. However, although the service may have quietened down the activity for a while (or even been successful in releasing the spirit of old lady), as recently as March 1992, the Hall was again in the papers after more spooky happenings!

The Manchester Metro News carried an article about the security guards working in and around the Hall, which had been closed down around 1990 by the North West Regional Health Authority. It was then put up for sale, but unfortunately fell victim to attacks by vandals, and therefore had to have a twenty four hour watch by guards and dogs, just to protect the Grade two listed building.

It was during the night shift that the ghost made its presence known, and frightened the security guards working there. One of the guards, 61 year old Les Millington said he had seen the ghost of an old nurse wearing a Victorian-style bonnet, and had heard her crying. Four other guards also claimed to have heard her cries between 2am and 2.30am. Les also said that on one occasion his dog Rocky was rooted to the spot in fear, when the ghost appeared.

Apparently, the activity increased around Christmas-time when the windows were boarded up as protection from vandals.

This is quite common in my experience as a ghosthunter, when any alterations, even decorating, can spark off ghostly activity in a building. The noises and movement must disturb the spirits, or even annoy them if the place is being changed drastically from how they knew it in life.

The activity is still going on, as a friend of ours informed us, although there are reports of a young child now haunting the place.

Anyone who has seen the Hall, must admit that it is very striking, to say the least. Some buildings seem to have the amazing ability to store events, or feelings in their very walls – call it the *vibes* of the place if you wish. Mauldeth certainly seems to have this talent and consequently, any events which result in strong emotions (be they bad or good), are mysteriously recorded just like a video tape, and replayed to those sensitive enough to receive the "transmission".

It is now in the process of being converted to houses by a new, anonymous buyer. Part of the proposals include demolishing a large section of the building which has fallen victim to dry rot, and is presumably unsafe. As I mentioned earlier, any alterations, especially to this degree, are likely to spark off ghostly activity, so this case must remain open.

Bar Spirits

The Hoylake Hotel was haunted by an apparition which wore a tweed jacket and hat, and knickerbockers. This ghost walked through the bar and into the billiard room, witnessed by several customers, but if anyone gave chase it quickly disappeared. The costume certainly suggested that the ghost came from around the turn of the century, but no cause has been ascertained for the haunting.

The Unheeded Warning

This account was first related by Peter Travis in his book "In Search of the Supernatural", telling how one gentleman had an unusual experience in 1954, as he travelled home from work in Manchester. He lived in Macclesfield, and used a small moped for the long journey each day. One evening the weather was particularly dreadful, and he debated taking a short cut down Alderley Cross, instead if his normal route through Monks' Heath. He stopped the bike by a signpost to see if the mileage was indeed less along the supposed short cut. As he did so, he saw another man on a bike, who had stopped at the opening to the road, blocking his passage. He walked across to the stranger, but before he reached him, the man cycled away along the road to Monks' Heath.

Having decided against taking an unfamiliar route on such a dark night, he continued after the cyclist on the usual road. However, he didn't once see the stranger on the road, although the moped could obviously go much faster than a push bike.

This experience puzzled the man so much, that he related it to a colleague at work the next day. His workmate, Mrs. C., told him that the figure was a ghost that was protecting him from some unknown danger. Although not being able to explain the stranger's disappearance, he refused to believe that he had seen a ghost. He just didn't want to believe in anything like that. As a sort of test to himself, perhaps to prove that he wasn't frightened or intimidated, he decided to take the new route home that very night.

From the outset, several annoying things went wrong with his moped. The lights began to flash on and off at odd occasions, so being a very practical man, he called at a shop and replaced the bulbs, and also checked the wiring. He continued on his way until he reached the same crossroads. Here, he took the turning down Alderley Cross, and soon after the engine just gave up, and broke down completely. He was forced to push the moped uphill, intending to try a downhill start. The engine wasn't the only problem though. He noted with concern that the chain had broken loose, and there was no way he could fix it in such poor light. Unperturbed, he went ahead with his downhill start, and got the bike going. However, although the engine was now working, his front light began to flicker again and he lent over to see if his rear light was working. As he did so, he suddenly lost control of the moped again, and going downhill at such a speed, when a large bend came up, he crashed into the side of the road.

A few seconds later, he came to his senses and was relieved to have suffered only cuts and bruises. As he was contemplating how lucky he was not have been seriously injured or even killed, a car came speeding around the corner without warning. He pulled his legs in, and just missed being hit by inches. This shock was too much for him, and he shakily made his way home.

The following day at work, before he could utter a word of the previous night's shocking events, Mrs. C. admonished him for not taking her seriously, and said that she knew all about the incident last night. To this day, he has no idea how she knew about it before he had mentioned it.

Combermere Abbey

Combermere Abbey near Whitchurch, is reputedly haunted by a little girl who once lived there, and is supposed to foretell a death in the family. One account of a sighting of the ghost appeared in "All the Year Round" in 1870.

The niece of the Lord Combermere at that time, was staying at the Abbey before she was to be married. However, one morning as she was getting dressed, she suddenly saw the form of a little girl "dressed in a very quaint frock, with an odd little ruff round its neck". She stared at the pitiful looking child until it began to run around the bed in a distressed way. Concerned, she held her hand out to the girl, who instantly disappeared "apparently into the floor".

Shocked by her encounter, the niece ran to Lady Combermere's room, an asked for an explanation of the event. Lady Combermere related a story told to her by her husband, which, she felt, accounted for the presence of the sad little girl.

Lord Combermere remembered playing with his sister one evening, when he was very young, running around the bed in an excited way, just as the niece had described. The following morning though, he was told that his sister had died during the night. As if this shock wasn't enough for a child, he was taken to see the laid out corpse. As the sheet was removed, he saw the blank face of his sister which had such an horrific impression upon him that he never forgot the scene, even in old age.

Whether or not the sighting of the apparition was followed by a death in the family, as the legend suggested, is not clear.

Soon after this account, the Abbey was put up for sale, and remained unsold for many years. The locals of the time, according to Fletcher Moss, declared that this was because the place was so haunted, although a lack of finance (it must have been a tidy sum that was needed to purchase such a property) was probably a more important factor.

However, Moss also related tales of ghostly monks who rose with the darkness to look in through the windows of the property, and scare any onlookers half to death. The monks were described as "grisly spectres...with lack-lustre eyes", who emitted frightful moaning and sighing sounds; not the most pleasant of encounters one could expect at such a late hour!

It is also said that the cowled forms of long-dead monks were seen floating around in the mist near the mere itself, and that more still haunted the site of their own graves in the area where the cloisters once stood.

Unfortunately, there have been no accounts that I have heard from this century, but of course, there's still time!

Opposite: the Combermere monks

6

Hideous Apparition at Ashley Hall

This account was first brought to my attention when I was just thirteen, and being introduced to the subject of ghosts by a series of books by Aidan Chambers. It concerns Ashley Hall near the River Bollin, and tells of a rather fearful looking "White Lady" who haunted the Cedar Room. The story comes from a lady who was in contact with the Merediths who lived in the Hall for many years. Her name was not revealed, but to help the readers, I shall give her a fictitious name – Karen.

Ashley Hall

As a young girl, Karen went to stay at the Hall with her friend Miss Meredith, and was also a good friend of her mother, Mrs. Meredith. On one occasion, there were so many guests staying that an old room had to be opened to accommodate her. The Cedar Room was not so much a bedroom, as a connecting room, with doors in every wall leading to various parts of the house. It was a very pleasant, bright room though, with large windows and an attractive fireplace.

On the first night, she went to bed feeling very tired, and was asleep in no time. Suddenly though, between two and three in the morning, she awoke with a start and saw the figure of a woman moving across the room. Annoyed at this intrusion of privacy, she called out to the stranger, but received no answer. The figure crossed the room and seemed to disappear into the door. However, it was quite dark, and Karen rationalised the whole thing, deciding it was probably a guest, unsure of the layout of the house, who maybe had too much to drink, and was too embarrassed to acknowledge the indiscretion. But when morning arrived, and she went down to breakfast, she realised that the doors had been securely locked all night, and had no idea how a stranger could have gained entry.

At the breakfast table, she enquired of her hostess Mrs. Meredith, who the stranger could have been. Mrs. Meredith seemed rather concerned, but did not say anything. It seemed to Karen that she was holding something back.

The following night she went to bed a little earlier, and was sound asleep when again at around 2am she was woken mysteriously. The same apparition was in the room, but this time Karen could see the face. It was not a pretty sight. She described her as "pale, with large, melancholy, black eyes", and noticed that her feet made no sound upon the bare oak floor as she moved. She stood in front of her for what seemed like an eternity, leaving Karen feeling absolutely petrified, and prevented her sleeping any longer that night. During the long hours of darkness, she decided to leave the house as soon as morning arrived, or at least demand to be moved to another room. However, when morning did arrive, the cold light of day chased away her fear, and made her realise how silly her story would sound to everyone else. She said nothing of her experience, and decided to stay.

As darkness fell once again, she felt more and more afraid of returning to the Cedar Room, and stayed up as late as possible to make sure the dreaded time – 2am – was long gone. She succeeded in this, and retired much later, checking the room thoroughly, especially the locks and bolts on the doors. She jumped into bed and hid her head under the covers for as long as she could possibly stand. After about two hours, dawn was breaking, and she felt sure she had missed the hideous spectre. Slowly, she pulled the covers down from her face to look around the room.

To her horror, the figure was looming just above her, inches away from touching her face! She stared straight into the "cavernous, black and melancholy eyes" and became paralysed in terror. She felt so vulnerable and threatened by this unearthly visitor that she fainted, and did not come around until almost noon.

She went downstairs looking very pale, and decidedly ill. Mrs. Meredith noticed this change immediately, and asked what was wrong. The whole story came flooding out, and Mrs. Meredith listened in silence, then apologised sincerely. Apparently, she had heard tales before but not believed them. She asked Karen to keep quiet about the whole thing though, in case the other guests were frightened off. She agreed, but despite Mrs. Meredith's protests, left just a few hours later.

Her next visit was not until many years later, when Mrs. Meredith's sister, Lady Pierrepont, was also staying, with her three children. Being a Lady who always got her own way, Lady Pierrepont insisted that the Cedar Room be opened up for her children to sleep in. Mrs. Meredith could not dissuade her, nor tell her of the ghost for fear of being ridiculed. To her relief though, two weeks passed by without incident, and she began to think that perhaps three boisterous children had frightened the ghost off.

However, one day, she found the children packing away their toys as if to leave. She questioned them, and received the following answer... "..we are going to hide our toys from the White Lady. She came last night and Sunday night, and she had such large black eyes and she stood close by the bed."

Mrs. Meredith quickly had the children moved to another room, despite their mother's protestations, declaring "this White Lady will be the death of me". With that, the room was shut up, and not used for many years, until her son had a large birthday party, and the space was again needed to accommodate everyone.

With the frivolities of the party on her mind, Mrs. Meredith cheerfully went into the Cedar Room to change. As she was stood in front of a full length mirror, the ghastly apparition of the White Lady materialised beside her! She collapsed in terror, and became very ill. It was an illness from which she never recovered, and as Karen attended the funeral, she could not help recalling the words " this White Lady will be the death of me".

An interesting final word to this story can be provided by T.A. Coward, who affirmed the presence of a White Lady in Ashley Hall in his 1932 publication, "Cheshire". He remembered tales of the ghost from years before, but said that the Lady had probably "retired" because no more accounts had been forthcoming. Even so, he told of some cab-men (notoriously sceptical in his opinion) that had seen the White Lady on several occasions.

The Spook Light

The Tiviot Hotel in Stockport town centre has had an interesting ghost in its cellars. The story was reported in 1958, when the licensee was a Mrs. Lillian Haslam, who lived-in with her husband Charles and eleven year old son, Melvin.

It was Mr. Haslam who first encountered something in 1956, two years before. He was working in the cellar, and moved into a corner to get something when he suddenly felt extremely cold, an icy cold which was "...much more intense than any other part of the cellars" he said. However, he continued with his work, dismissing the incident completely, until a few minutes later his attention was again drawn to the same corner. This time, he saw something. "It was just like a bluish, flickering light," he said, "I watched it for about a minute before it faded and vanished. It had no particular shape, and was about two feet long." He went towards it to investigate, but could find nothing to explain what he had seen.

The Tiviot Hotel

After this incident, he began to see the same shape regularly. On the fourth occasion, he made a rush for it, and it retreated towards a tunnel entrance, and disappeared. The tunnel was rumoured to lead all the way from the cellars to Lyme Park! Mr. Haslam then entered the tunnel and saw the shape again, just as before, and about three yards away from him. Again he went towards it, but it just disappeared. This had happened several times, and it always vanished in the same spot.

Lillian Haslam said she had also seen the ghost, and felt the extreme cold in the cellar, but their son Melvin saw nothing, although he admitted feeling uneasy in the cellars.

In December 1958, a reporter and camera-man from the Stockport Express, actually accompanied Mr. Haslam down to the cellars to see if they could experience this spook light for themselves. They were not to be disappointed!

The three of them went into the old tunnel, and stood in the exact spot where the ghost had been seen. They waited nervously, and waited ... and waited. After half an hour in the same spot, they began to feel as if the journey had been a waste of time, and decided to call it a day. They were making their way out of the tunnel, when suddenly they saw something just in front of, and above them! They described it as a "...faint, flickering light, slightly blue in colour and of no definite shape." It remained near the roof, hovering in the same spot, and actually seemed to grow stronger after a few minutes. "There it is," said Mr. Haslam, "exactly as I have seen it in the past." With that, he again moved towards it, and they all watched it fade and then disappear altogether.

The ghost always appeared late at night/early morning, but was very unpredictable. Sometimes, Mr. Haslam said, he could see it two or three times a week, and yet other times he would only see it say, once in ten days. When asked if he was frightened, he said "I'm not scared by it at all. The only thing that bothers me is not knowing what it is, what causes it and where it comes from. I'll find out one day, I suppose."

During 1993 I investigated this case with my fellow ghosthunter Martin Mills. The pub changed hands in 1968, and the present licensee told us of another incident he and some of his bar staff had experienced over the years. Again, the activity was confined to the cellar area, which is accessible through a trap door behind the bar. The licensee, Dave, explained how one day a member of staff opened the trap door as usual, but before they could reach for the light switch, they distinctly saw a ghostly face staring back at them from the steps! It appeared to be the face of a young child. This was backed up by a incident in the pub's history where a mother and child were killed on those very steps, presumably from a fall, because the entrance to the cellar is very steep.

Following this information, we later conducted a ghost tour of several pubs in Stockport town centre, including the Tiviot. No activity was reported on the evening, but when we returned there the following week we were told that a playful poltergeist had started interfering with the daily running of the pub. In that one week, the gas taps to the pumps behind the bar had been switched off by a mysterious hand in the cellar. No one else had been around at these times to have played a joke on Dave, and he had to go down into the cellar to manually turn the taps back on again.

This happened several more times, and in early October, myself and five other people conducted an all-night ghosthunt in the cellars of the pub. Whilst directly below the bar area I heard some very light but fast footsteps, which sounded like those of a child. Upon investigation upstairs, there was nothing to be seen. The pub was in fact closed and securely locked, the only other person inside being the landlord Dave who was asleep on the first floor. Another member of the group heard three heavy footsteps walking towards her, but as the lights were out, she could see nothing. The steps seemed to stop directly in front of her, but when we switched on the torches, there was no one to be seen, and none of the other members of the group (who were all wearing trainers and could not have made such loud footsteps) had moved. Several loud bangs and crashes were heard emanating from the cellar door whilst we were down there, and also from upstairs on the ground floor, although cause could be found for the noises.

14

About a fortnight after the vigil, Martin and I were conducting more ghost tours in the cellar, and on one particular occasion, a member of the public had a nose stud mysteriously ripped from her nose! None of the crowd had pulled or caught the stud, or been near enough to the lady at the time of the incident, and when retrieved from the floor, the gold stud was found to have been bent out of shape. The lady took it to a jewellers shop, but the assistant said it was impossible to fix.

Not much is known of the history of the building, except that it was once called The Horseshoe, and in 1830 the landlord was tragically killed by an explosion of gunpowder on the London Coach. His bereaved wife left the pub in 1833. It is unlikely that this has anything to do with the ghost in the cellars, but you can never be sure. At the time of writing, this case is definitely not closed, with little incidents of poltergeist activity being constantly brought to my attention.

Tragedy at Tabley

Tabley Old Hall is the site of a rather interesting story, which explains the presence of two ghosts, who appear leaning over the balustrade.

The tale began many years ago, when the resident family of the time had a large gathering. One guest started to become extremely jealous when he imagined that another man was spending too much time with his wife. He became so enraged that he challenged the offender to a duel. However, this did not work to his advantage, and he was killed by his opponent. His wife was so horrified and distraught that she took her own life shortly afterwards.

Being the local manor house, it was imperative that the family avoided a scandal kept their good name. As a consequence, the two bodies were unceremoniously walled up inside the house, or so the legend says. Romantic though the tale is, it could explain the appearance of the two ghosts who might be trying to attract attention to their unconsecrated resting place.

Curse of the Mummy's Hand

A strange account comes from Bowden around the turn of the century. One lady had spent several years abroad in Egypt, and returned with a rather grisly memento of her trip – a genuine mummy's hand. To go with the relic went an inevitable curse, but being a sensible woman, she dismissed the natives superstitions thinking that they were just trying to frighten her. The object became a prized possession, and she placed it in a glass case in her drawing room, to display to all her visitors. However, she had not been back long when the curse appeared to start making itself apparent. She spent many sleepless nights listening to strange and frightening noises, which seemed to emanate from the drawing room. Upon investigation, she could find no obvious cause for the sounds, and nothing in the room had been tampered with. After many nights of these disturbances, she became uneasy and remembered the curse. Without further ado, the next evening she quietly took the hand from the case and made her way to the nearest graveyard. Armed with just a spoon, she dug a hole and buried the cursed relic, hoping to give the long-dead owner some peace. The problems in her house immediately stopped, but the tale may not have ended there as she was watched by several boys near the graveyard. They dug the hand up after she had left, but no one knows what happened to it, or the boys after that.

Spectral Encounters at Lyme

Lyme Hall in Disley is well known for its ghostly guests, which include a White Lady and a full funeral procession. Built in 1541 by Sir Piers Legh VII, the Hall stands on the site of an earlier home which dated back to 1465. Little is left of the Sixteenth Century design, following extensive alteration (including some demolition and reconstruction) in the Eighteenth Century.

The ghostly funeral procession dates from the earlier building however, after Sir Piers Legh II died from wounds inflicted in battle, some say from Agincourt, but this is debatable according to researchers who disagree upon the actual date of his death. What-ever the date, his body was buried at Lyme in what is known as "Knight's Low", and even today there have been reports of a host of mourning spectres travelling from the Hall to "Knight's Low", with the body of Sir Piers at the head. Witnesses are apparently warned of this procession by loud wailing cries from a White Lady with the group. Again legend has blurred the story because there are two versions of the White Lady's identity. One says that it is the young daughter Blanche, so heavily grieved by her father's death that she soon after drowned herself in the River Bollin. A more romantic version suggests that Blanche was in fact a young woman from the Hall, unrelated to Sir Piers but very much in love with him, and jealous of his wife Lady Joan. When he died, Blanche could find no other reason to live and also took her own life.

The next accounts of supernatural activity are also attributed to Lady Blanche, who died in 1422, but I find this hard to believe in my experience as a ghosthunter, because the White Lady who haunts the Hall is what is termed as an Historic Ghost, (one who returns to places they knew in life like a recorded image, and is often unaware of any onlookers). Lady Blanche would have known the Hall in an earlier design, seeing as the present one was constructed in 1541 (not counting the alterations in the 1700s). This suggests that the sightings of the White Lady I am about to relate, are of a different, but equally interesting phantom.

The sightings of this mysterious lady all come from the same area of the Hall, that of an old booth which now houses a public telephone. One evening in 1985 a painter who was working late in the building, finished making a personal phone call and was stunned to see a lady dressed in white walk past him. He turned around to see where she had gone, but could see no one. The lady had disappeared! A similar thing happened to another painter not long afterwards, but this time, she made her appearance in the early morning. This painter had also finished his conversation and actually stepped out of the booth, when the White Lady walked past him. As he saw the figure, he said "Good morning", presum-ably thinking it was an early visitor to the Hall, but something in her manner made him curious, and he turned around to look at her, but again she had disappeared. In 1988, a new employee had a memorable welcome to the Hall, by first being snowed-in, and forced to spend the night there. He decided to telephone his wife at home and tell her of his predicament, but as he opened the door to the phone booth, the White Lady walked out of it! The man said that she did not made him feel frightened in any way, just curious.

Lyme Hall

Mary, Queen of Scots, is also reputed to haunt Lyme, from the time she was held prisoner there by Elizabeth I. She had been allowed to move to Lyme because of her poor health, so that she could sample the spa water of Buxton in an effort to relieve her rheumatism. The room itself is very atmospheric, with dark wood panelling, crooked walls and ceiling, rounded off with the original black four poster bed that Mary was said to have slept in.

In April 1988 Jean Coulthurst, the caretaker's wife was walking down the hallway on her way to meet a party of visitors she was to show around the Hall. However, as she passed the Mary Queen of Scots' room, she was suddenly struck by a very powerful odour, that of oranges. There was no one else around, and she could not think where this "psychic odour" had come from. When she met the group of visitors, she took them on the regular tour, and when she reached the spooky room, she mentioned her recent experience. To her surprise, one of the visitors stated that it must have been the ghost of Mary herself, because the lady had actually invented marmalade, although in her time she used it as a cure for her chest problems.

Apart from its eerie atmosphere, several people have come out of the room, feeling as if there had been someone else in there with them, although they do not think it was Mary. It has been suggested that they could have sensed the presence of a very unfortunate priest whose body was found many years ago, sealed up under the floorboards. Identification of this skeleton was impossible, but it is thought that it was a frightened priest hiding from the authorities, who had starved to death and been forgotten.

The Cage, Lyme Hall

Many rumours surround what is known as "the Cage", a large and very eerie sort of watch-tower which is situated along the road leading up to the Hall. "The Cage Chronicle" by Kate Atkinson was published in June 1989 by the owners of Lyme Park, and relates a fascinating, and well documented tale from 1903, concerning the residents of the cage at that time. The shepherd from the park, Joseph Morten was finding life in the cage rather disturbing, as he and his family often encountered an unwanted visitor – the ghost of the White Lady mentioned earlier. Apparently, the ghost would appear every evening after the children had been put to bed. The residents did not seem frightened by this, but had understandably become fed up with nightly intrusion on their privacy, so much so that they requested to be moved to a more peaceful house. The article related how Lord Newton understood their problem, and was willing to let them move to the "Little Lodge" on Red Lane. The Cage has been unoccupied for many years and is now considerably dilapidated, but the striking outline of the building is still a sign synonymous with Lyme Park and its fascinating history.

2

More Cheshire Ghosts

"Mockbeggar Hall"

Leasowe Castle on Merseyside was built in 1593 for the Earl of Derby, but eventually fell into disrepair and disrepute, being renamed "Mockbeggar Hall". It was used as a private house, a hostel for shipwrecked sailors, and eventually a hotel. It was during its span as a hotel that guests began to report the presence of two ghosts.

One visitor was shocked to see a man and boy stood at the end of his bed, even though he was alone in the room with the door locked. Several guests also heard ghostly footsteps on the stairs, and other strange sounds, although there was no one there who could have caused the disturbances.

Unfortunately, financial problems forced the hotel to close, and the building changed hands yet again to become the Railwaymens' Convalescent Home. Whether or not the new occupants experienced anything unusual, was not reported. However, there is a legend surrounding the place, that could explain the presence of the two sorrowful apparitions.

It is said that many years ago, a family feud involved Leasowe Castle in a tragedy. A father and son were captured as leaders of one side of the feud, and were imprisoned in one of the castle's rooms. With the promise of torture and imprisonment, the father decided to spare himself and his son a long and painful death, and so killed his son, and then himself by dashing his brains out on the stone wall.

After such a gruesome tragedy, it is little wonder that there are unsettled spirits in this particular building.

Leasowe Castle

The Sad Spectre at Thurstaston

A very reliable witness to a haunting in Thurstaston Hall, was actually able to make a sketch of his nightly visitor.

The witness was an artist who was staying temporarily with friends at the Hall who had recently moved in. He was given a comfortable room, and settled in well. However, during the night, he was surprised to see a little old lady enter the room. She appeared to be in great distress by the way she was wringing her hands. She stood at the end of his bed, and being a sensible man, he realised that she meant him no harm, but in fact needed help herself. With no reason to be afraid, he gently asked the lady if he could do anything to help her. Unfortunately she seemed totally oblivious to his presence (what could probably be termed an

22

historic ghost), and crossed the room to the bell-rope, which she pulled, and then suddenly disappeared.

This sad routine continued each night, so the artist decided to make a sketch of the pitiful wretch, and hopefully identify her. This he did very successfully, and showed it to the friends he was staying with. They had no idea who the woman was, and were not even aware of any rumours of a ghost anywhere in the Hall.

Determined to solve the mystery, the sketch was shown to a former owner of the Hall who immediately recognised it as one of his ancestors. To reinforce his statement, he even mentioned that the lady's portrait used to hang in the Hall, and that was how he recognised her. Unfortunately, that was as far as he could go, for no scandal was known to surround the woman, and they were unable to explain her sad fate.

Tragedy of a Forbidden Passion

This tale seems to be more of a legend than anything else as it was recorded a long time ago, and there is no trace of such a haunting now. However, all legends are born of fact, no matter how little, so who knows?

It concerns a small manor near Chester, where the monks of St Werburgh were said to have quarried the rock for some of the stones to build Chester Cathedral. The foreman of the estate had a very beautiful daughter, who caught the eye of the workers' overseer, also a "man of the cloth". It is said that the cleric, overcome with passion, raped the girl and in a fit of guilt and shame, murdered her and buried her close to a nearby stream next to a beech tree. As time passed, the tree had to be cut down to accommodate a new house, and a human skeleton was discovered.

It was said that for many years, the apparitions of a priest and a woman could be seen under the tree. A passer-by also heard three sighs emanate from the ground beneath his feet, and when he walked back to the house, he saw what appeared to be a drowning woman. He hurried to the stream to rescue her but could find no trace of anyone having been there.

It is not clear how much of the tale is true, but it is possible that the area has some supernatural activity to spark off such tales.

The Combermere Arms

Spirit Trapped in a Bottle

The Combermere Arms at Burleydam near Whitchurch was taken over by Chris Wright in 1984, who set to work refurbishing the pub. In doing so, he apparently disturbed a dormant spirit who made its noisy presence well known!

During the first six months of renovations, the workers found their jobs hindered by a whole host of problems. The climax to it all seemed to come in November 1984, when the resident manager Maurice Wright was abruptly woken up in the night by a hard thumping under his bed. There was no one around to have played

24

such a curious joke, and their pet Alsatian lay undisturbed and fast asleep.

It is said that the perpetrator of this, and many other mischievous pranks, was a spirit that had been trapped in a bottle by two priests, and buried underneath the pub's front steps. Supposedly, it could only return if it was disturbed. It is an original and interesting account of what most haunted pubs normally term 'poltergeist' activity.

Mischievous Children

During the 1970s, a former school in Warrington witnessed the return of some ghostly children. For about seven days in a row, the building which had been converted to a shop had embarrassing urine puddles on the floor. No logical explanation could be found for their origin, as their were no animals, no leaks in the roof, and the shop was locked securely every night. However, each morning, the puddle would appear again, and dry out through the day, leaving a white stain on the floor.

This was not all though, on one occasion a witness actually saw the urine being produced from about eighteen inches high, and arc down to form the puddle. Again, there were no leaks or pipes which could have accounted for this circumstance.

One customer became concerned by the ghostly goings-on, and being very religious, she offered to go home and pray for the lost spirits. She got more than she bargained for however, and was followed by the ghost, which soaked her bed with urine that very night!

There is no information relating to why it suddenly started, or when, if ever, it stopped. Ghosts are very individual creatures and react to things in their own way, with some very strange results!

A Kindly Visitor

A brief account comes from what was the old Quay House near Parkgate on the Wirral, which described a very friendly spirit. Built in the early Sixteenth Century, it had a varied history, being known as a "waterside tavern" and later spell as a prison. In 1759 it was up for rental to travellers on their way to and from Ireland.

In the 1870's the house was bought by an artist and yachtsman named Henry Melling, who lived with his invalid niece, Clara Payne. She led a frustrating life, being confined to bed from her illness, but was frequently cheered up by a ghostly visitor; an old woman dressed in a red cloak. She would come in and warm herself by the fire, keeping the girl company, and occasionally sitting by her bedside. Suddenly though, the visitations ceased, no one knows why, but Clara was greatly distressed by the loss of her mysterious friend, who instead of frightening the girl, had come in love and friendship in the invalid's hours of loneliness.

Henry Melling of course tried to determine the identity of this kindly old ghost, but could find no more than a few clues. As mentioned previously, the house had once been a prison, and an inn, and either of these could have seen some dastardly deed which would suggest the presence of the ghost. Alternatively, the lady could have been attracted by the girl's plight, and sought to help the invalid, acting as a sort of guardian spirit.

Apparition of Conscience

In the days before modern transport allowed virtually secure travelling, many merchants and travellers disappeared without trace, and came to some rather grisly ends. Such a tale concerns an inn on the Higher Town Common in Knutsford.

A rent-collector, weary from his journey, stopped at the inn for rest and refreshment. However, the landlord spied the man's rather large bag of money, and greed overtook his sensibilities. He murdered the man, and buried him in a sand-hole nearby. He took the money and continued his life without ever being suspected of such a mercenary crime.

But, as time passed, his conscience began to ache, further encouraged by the restless spirit of the rent-collector. Each time the landlord passed the sand-hole where the body had been buried, he saw the hideous ghost coming towards him. This continued for the rest of his life, until at last, on his death-bed, he admitted everything to unbelieving listeners. No one had any idea before then of the ghastly truth, but the ghost of the rent-collector demanded recognition, and got it.

"The Devil's Bell?"

A very romantic tale is told of Rostherne Mere, which is supposed to echo with the ghostly ringing of a bell each Easter morning.

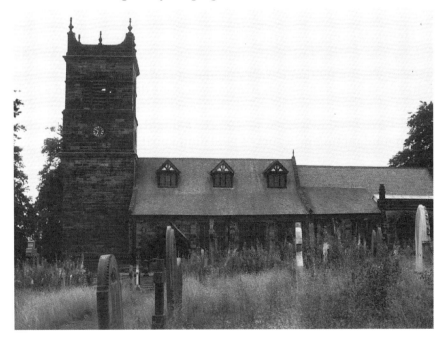

Rostherne Church

27

The legend behind this is that when the village church had new bells hung, one of them (the largest) persistently came loose, and fell down towards the mere. After three times of dragging the heavy item back, and re-hanging it, the workmen understandably became fed up with the situation. The next time the bell broke loose, one of the men kicked it, and cursed it. The minute he said that, the bell rolled into the mere where it disappeared for ever, chiming an eerie note.

A similar legend is told of the Combermere bells, but on this occasion, the blaspheming workman was carried off with the bell to the murky depths of the mere. A variation on this tells of how a demonic apparition rose from the water, and actually dragged the man and bell down together.

The eerie chiming of the Rostherne bell is supposed to still haunt the mere, when the ghostly form of a mermaid is said to rise each Easter and chime the bell as a prelude to her sweet song.

Rostherne Mere

The Phantom Priest

Another strange tale to come from around the turn of the century, is from an area called Neston.

When the local Catholic priest was absent, a lady called Theresa Higginson had possession of the keys to the church. One morning she saw a priest enter whom she didn't recognise. She followed him into the church, and he signalled to her without speaking, that he would like to say Mass. Theresa saw no harm in this as she noticed that he seemed to know his way around the place anyway.

This went ahead as normal, and then he entered the vestry. After a few minutes, Theresa could hear nothing, and wondered if everything was all right. She also went into the vestry, and was completely bewildered when she found it empty. There was no other exit, and she had definitely not seen him come out. This only happened the once, but so puzzled her that she mentioned it to the Bishop. Upon hearing her description of the man, he appeared startled, and had to admit that it was the same description of a former priest of the parish, who had died and was buried in that very churchyard.

Ghostly Horseman

In 1934, Orchard House in Lower Bebington was demolished, and with it disappeared the mysterious secret of a phantom horse.

On many occasions, and with several reliable witnesses present, the sound of a hastily galloping horse was heard charging to the gates of the driveway, and then stopping suddenly. Many times, baffled listeners raced to the gates to find the cause of the commotion, but never found anything to account for it – not even hoofprints. The mystery was never solved, and probably never will be.

The White Lady of Marbury Hall

Marbury Hall near Northwich was demolished in 1968 because of its terrible state of disrepair. The gardens and park are still open to the public, and if you traverse the grounds, bear in mind this spooky story concerning the Hall itself.

The story concerns a beautiful foreign lady who married into the Barrymore family which lived in the Hall at the time. Unfortunately, she didn't live long, and her last request was to be buried inside the Hall, which she had fallen in love with. The coffin was buried underneath the main staircase, but as generations passed, the occupants of the house began to feel uneasy with the presence of a corpse under the stairs. Eventually, the wishes of the new generation prevailed, and the coffin was moved to the nearby St Mary and All Saints Church.

This blatant contradiction of the lady's last wish, caused incredible uproar in the Hall. The unhappy spirit returned to express her disapproval of the move, by disturbing the residents with loud noises and thumps during the night. The service bells were rung by an invisible hand, and the family plagued by annoying poltergeist activity. It wasn't long before the body was exhumed and replaced under the stairs!

Again, time passed, and the Hall changed hands, bringing a new family with no knowledge of the legend whatsoever. Consequently, as the years passed the body was discovered, and acting in what they thought was the unknown skeleton's best interests, it was again removed to the churchyard and buried ceremoniously. The family were shocked therefore when the ghostly activity resumed, and disturbed them night and day. As a result, the coffin was again replaced under the stairs. There it remained until the 1930s.

It is not clear exactly what happened to it during the thirties, but some German prisoners during the Second World War claimed to have seen the apparition of a White Lady. After the war I.C.I. took possession of the building, and there were no reports of any ghostly activity. Rumour has it that the coffin now lies underneath the Rose Garden, a successful compromise perhaps on both sides?

Shocklach Parish Church

A Ghostly Get-Together

Shocklach Parish Church is reputed to have a large ghostly gathering once a year. The Brereton family are said to rise from their graves, and travel to the church in coaches (also apparitions). Lucky witnesses claim that the once powerful family are revisiting their old territory, although why this should happen once a year, is not clear.

The Cheerful Children of Hale

This story comes with the kind permission of Vivienne Rae-Ellis from her book "True Ghost Stories Of Our Own Time". The events took place several years ago in a large Victorian house in Hale, and were related to Ms Ellis by the witness Mrs. Margaret Maguire.

One evening at about half past ten, Margaret was alone in the house, her family all being out, and was rather puzzled therefore to hear the sounds of several children singing. She opened the door to see if anyone was outside, but there was no one there.

The sound seemed to emanate from the third floor of the house, the attic room, which was only used for storage, and was very rarely entered. The singing continued for about ten minutes, and then faded away. She said she was not afraid because the voices sounded so happy and cheerful, but nevertheless, she didn't investigate the incident until the following day, when she of course found the room exactly the same as before. She didn't tell anyone of her experience for fear of being ridiculed, and never heard the sounds again, so felt no need to involve the family, who may have become frightened.

Several months later, the family had some friends round, and their conversation wandered onto the subject of the supernatural. Margaret was surprised to hear her daughter declare their house was haunted, and questioned her thoroughly, without admitting at first that she believed her. The daughter, Mary, repeated the story of her encounters which matched perfectly with that of her mother's experience. Margaret then had to admit that she had also heard the ghostly singing.

No cause for this was ever discovered, and as far as I can tell, nothing further has been experienced there yet.

Dastardly Deeds at Dutton

Dutton Hall which dates from the early Sixteenth Century, was once a very notable residence ; "a mansion of no mean importance in the days of Henry VIII", as T.A. Coward put it. Built by Sir Piers Dutton, two inscriptions in the porch and doorway bear the dates 1539, and 1542. An item of controversy at the time of building was that the Hall was supposed to have used materials which had been looted from Norton Priory after its dissolution.

T.A. Coward paid a visit to the Hall himself when he was researching for "Picturesque Cheshire", and found that the owners at the time were so afraid of the Hall's ghost that a whole room had been sealed up, and the entrance papered over in the gallery. Rumour has it that the spectre is that of an old soldier, although why he was bound to return, or how he died, is not known. Nevertheless, it must have been a fearsome sight that led to such a drastic action as sealing off the room.

Frightened to Death by a Prince!

The Old Parsonage in Handforth is rumoured to be haunted by the ghost of a woman who died after receiving a great shock. Presumably, the lady must have had a weak heart because her reaction was extreme to say the least. During 1745, Bonnie Prince Charlie paid a visit to Handforth Hall, and whilst in the area, decided to look in on the householders of the Parsonage. The aforementioned lady opened the door to his Majesty, and was so shocked that he was there in person, that she instantly collapsed and died. Her restless spirit is said to return to the scene, but luckily she has not had the same effect on the new witnesses, as the Prince's appearance had on her!

Authorley's Exorcist

Fletcher Moss revealed that Authorley had been victim to a rather fearsome haunting, although no date was mentioned. The spirit of an old gamekeeper used to frighten away any passers-by, and to make things worse, he was accompanied by a ghostly black dog. Residents of Authorley became so worried by these apparitions that they called upon the help of the local parson. The brave man left one night to tackle the supernatural trouble-causers, but must have encountered more than he bargained for. In the course of that one night, his jet black hair had turned completely grey! Nevertheless, he apparently had managed to release the spirit, and gained a great deal of respect from his parishioners.

Capesthorne's Collection of Spectres

Capesthorne Hall would not be complete without its traditional ghosts, and traditional they certainly are. Built in 1719 by the Smith's of Warwick, it is still used as a family home by the Bromley-Davenports, whose ancestors are well noted in the annals of Cheshire's history. Disaster struck in 1861 though, in the form of a terrible fire, which destroyed much of the centre section. The skilled reconstruction of Anthony Salvin, allowed the Hall to return to its former glory, and continue to impress visitors even today.

With such a grand setting and so much historical interest, one cannot be surprised by the tales of a ghostly Grey Lady, who has been seen by several reliable witnesses. Sir Charles Taylor M.P. was just one of these, and encountered her on a visit to the Hall. One evening, he heard the rustle of long skirts behind him, and turned around curiously to see where this noise was coming from. To his surprise, he saw the ghost of a lady dressed in grey, with her long skirts trailing behind her as she walked along the corridor below him. It lasted for just a few seconds, and then disappeared without trace.

Capesthorne Hall

Sir Walter was also witness to a more startling display of supernatural activity. On the 250th anniversary of the building of the family's private chapel, he saw an array of ghosts descending the steps which lead to the family vault. He remarked at the time "I presume they are my ancestors, and so whenever they have appeared I have had the spot blessed by the church, and I hope they are now laid to rest."

Perhaps the most frightening of the family's experiences is that of Sir Walter's son, William. He was woken up abruptly one night in 1958 by a severe rattling sound from his window. He got up to see what was going on, and couldn't believe his eyes when he saw a disembodied arm moving the frame with some force! As he attempted to open the securely fastened window, the hideous apparition disappeared. He looked outside and could see nothing,

35

after all the room was thirty feet above the ground! Ever since, it has been nicknamed The Room with the Severed Arm.

No origin has ever been discovered for this apparition, or that of the Grey Lady, so their presence remains a mystery. Capesthorne Hall is open to the public, so you can seek them out for yourself!

A Gruesome Scene from the Past

One of the most memorable accounts I have heard, has to be that of the two apparitions Dave Warham saw in Curzon Park, Chester. Charles Fairclough related the story in his book "Chester Ghosts and Poltergeists". It began in November 1984, when Dave was returning home late at night, and heard the sound of a woman crying. Concerned for this lady's safety, he stopped and looked around to see if he could find the cause, and help in some way. As he turned, he saw in front of him the form of a woman in Tudor or Elizabethan dress, with her head bowed in her hands in sorrow. The reason for her distress however, took Dave completely by surprise, for just to her side was a man hanging by his neck from a tree! Shocked by this horrific apparition, it took him a few minutes to move and make his way home as fast as possible. As he did so, the scene disappeared.

He related this tale to his parents, who saw how distressed he was, but advised him to keep it quiet, so as not to upset anyone. He agreed to this, and even began to doubt what he had seen. That was until the same time the following night, when he saw the same gruesome spectacle! There was no doubt this time, or the next, for he saw it again for a third time soon after.

It was suggested that he had "picked up" a recorded image from many years ago, just as a lot of people are able to "tune in" to the other side.

Phantoms at Farndon

It is well noted that Farndon Bridge has a sad history, and is haunted as the result of two men's' greed. During the early Fourteenth Century, it is said that after Prince Madoc died he left his two young sons in the care of Roger Mortimer and the Earl of Warren. Driven by an incredible desire to possess the late Prince's valuable property and possessions, they took the two boys to the old stone bridge at Farndon, which links England and Wales, and threw them off to certain death in the freezing, murky waters below.

The murder did not go unnoticed though, because from then on, anyone crossing the bridge on stormy nights was likely to hear the terrified cries of the two boys drowning, and even their small white ghosts have been seen around the arches of the bridge.

Farndon Bridge

The Spectres at Poulton-Lancelyn

The Hall of Poulton-Lancelyn on the Wirral boasts a fascinating legend, and its consequent ghosts. The story goes that one Christmas Eve in the Eighteenth Century, a beautiful young nun became stranded by bad weather, and made her way to the Hall which was the closest shelter she could find. What she did not know though, was that the Squire had a terrible reputation, and consequently tried to seduce her. Loyal to her vows, she tried desperately to resist his advances, but this did not deter him. He told her that she could either submit to his desires, or become a prisoner and starve to death.

She still refused his advances, and was locked in a freezing room, all alone for many days. Eventually the evil Squire unlocked the door, and discovered her lifeless body, frozen and starved to death. Shocked by the results of his wiles, he made his way to the library and hanged himself.

The ghosts of both the nun and the Squire are said to haunt the Hall. One lady, an experienced psychic investigator, was left alone in the library for just a few minutes, and became greatly distressed, having "tuned in" to the restless spirit of the Squire.

A few years later, Ann Lake and her husband were invited to the Hall. Neither of them had any knowledge of the turbulent history, which makes Ann's experiences all the more fascinating. Having been left alone for a few minutes in an upstairs corridor, she was patiently waiting for her hostess to return, and moved back a little way into a recess between two doors. Suddenly, she was overcome with the powerful feeling of intense fear, and had the desire to escape at once. So marked was this that Ann actually began running downstairs. She soon came to her senses but could not shake the terrible feeling of being trapped.

Her story was related many years later, and she found out that the two doors she had been stood between were to the rooms in which the Squire, and the nun had died.

"Old Nanny"

Godley Green has had its share of paranormal activity. One farm had a ghost known as Old Nanny, whose apparition was seen wandering through the garden of her old home at dusk. She could also be seen occasionally by inhabitants of the farm, to be looking in at them through the windows. She was described as wearing a mob-cap, and having a "withered" face. One man saw her waving her apron, and uttering a strange hissing sound.

She was immediately identified by the family as the old lady who used to live there, although why she returned after her death was never discovered. Perhaps, as in many simple cases, she had been so fond of the place during her lifetime, that she did not want to leave, even after her death.

Godley Green Poltergeist

Another farm in Godley Green was home to a very mischievous poltergeist. Doors would open and close by themselves, or lock when no one was around. Disembodied footsteps were heard on the stairs, and the sound of someone sweeping the floor baffled everyone. Items were moved, or thrown on the floor, and the beds were rocked and stripped of covers.

So disturbing was all this activity, that the Pastor of Hyde, the Reverend James Brooks, was called in to quieten it down. He spent several nights in the haunted rooms, prayed and read the bible aloud with some success. The house was quiet for several months, but the disturbances gradually began again.

In the 1880s, children who lived there were shocked to see an old rocking chair moving to and fro, all by itself. They called in a farm hand to try and stop it, but he too was frightened, and wouldn't go near it. The farmer's wife heard of the commotion, and without further ado she sat down squarely in the chair, stopping it instantly. She said that the cause of the mysterious movement was a previous resident, an old lady who had died in that very rocking chair. Her ghost was frequently seen, she said, wandering around the house as if she was looking for something.

It is not clear if the incidents are connected, but some human bones were discovered in the garden, under a plot where nothing would grow.

In 1906, the same farm had another encounter with the super-natural. The farmer's wife was returning home one day along a road bordered by tall hedges. Although it was a still, calm day, the hedges suddenly began moving about, and the spectral figure of a woman in white stepped out from them, as if she was leaving the farm. The poor farmer's wife became extremely distressed, as her brother was seriously ill back at the farm. Upon her return she found that he had just passed away. Was the mysterious White Lady a final visitor to comfort him in his last moments? We'll never know.

The George and Dragon's Uninvited Guest

This traditional public house in Chester was built on the site of a Roman cemetery that was about 1,600 years old. This has obvi-ously inspired the conclusion that the ghost there is a Roman soldier. Footsteps were heard pacing to and fro along the upper floor of the pub, in the early morning. They were definitely not natural because the steps were heard walking the length of the floor, which actually has several solid brick walls running the width of it, which would block any normal person's progress.

The conclusion was reached that they had a ghost, and as it was the site of a Roman cemetery, that it must be a Roman ghost. However, if the ghost was walking through the walls in the attic, it would generally be assumed that was how the spirit would have known the building in life. It happens in many cases where the ghost is totally oblivious to human intervention. If that was the case, how could a Roman soldier returning to the site of the cemetery know the layout of the pub well enough to be able to walk along the attic, and make the sound of footfalls? It is more likely that the ghost is of a much more modern spirit, perhaps an old landlord/lady who knew the attic before the dividing walls were built.

However, it seems that the present tenants have heard nothing at all. This does not mean that the story is not true, just that the new tenants are not receptive to it. Just as with a radio, you have to be tuned in to the right wavelength, and everyone cannot be on the same one all the time, so you get ghosts felt/seen some of the time, by different people.

St Thomas' hospital and the old workhouse

Double Trouble at St Thomas's

During October 1974, the Stockport Express revealed that there had been many ghostly sightings at St Thomas's Hospital in Shaw Heath, Stockport. This only served to validate many rumours that already abounded in the town concerning this particular building. It started its life in 1841 as the town's workhouse, and soon had a bad name, as many workhouses did. Later this century it was converted to a hospital for elderly and terminally ill patients.

In 1974, several nurses of many years experience in the hospital related their stories. The ghost they spoke of was only ever seen at night, although it could be any night, and for varying lengths of time. Furthermore, it always appeared in exactly the same place. It was described as a woman of average height, attired in white robes (similar to a shroud), and seemed to emit a shining light. The apparition hovered a few feet above ground level, and appeared to be smiling at the onlookers.

One retired night sister who once worked at St Thomas's, claimed that when she first began her duties there, other nurses informed her of the spook. However, she believed it all to be the product of someone's fertile imagination, until she encountered the White Lady herself at 2am one morning, whilst doing her rounds. According to her, the ghost was solid in appearance, and never moved or spoke. It just hovered, perfectly still, constantly smiling.

The same sister also saw the mysterious figure on a few other occasions. Sometimes several nurses at once would encounter the ghost, while at other times it would be seen by a lone nurse.

Obviously, word soon started to spread. So much gossip began in fact, that pressure was applied to a former hospital superintendent, Mr. Wilfred Tattum, to organise an inquiry. Initially, he believed the phantom white lady to be no more than a projected image from Our Lady's church, of a statue or painting. Yet the "image", only ever appeared in an open area, with no background for a projection to utilize. Mr. Tattum's theories were therefore dashed, and after much puzzlement and little success, the investigation was dropped.

Of those nurses who saw the figure, some claimed that a visit from the White Lady was a portent of death at the hospital. This came from a noted coincidence between the appearance of the said ghost, and a subsequent fatality within the wards.

Later reports however, seemed to suggest that the White Lady was more caring than first suspected. To date, she has been seen by scores of nurses and patients, and has lately taken to visitations during the day as well as evening. The mother of a friend of mine related how a ghostly figure had been seen by the bedsides of dying patients, who had few visitors, and needed some comfort in their final hours. This lady also said that the White Lady was once encountered on a staircase inside the hospital. As a nurse was about to ascend the staircase, she was shocked to see the ghost coming down the steps, and then just walk past her.

Another apparition, nicknamed 'Old John' is said to haunt the geriatric ward. Late at night, he has been seen pacing the corridors in black, old fashioned clothing. Originally, witnesses believed him to be a visitor out of hours, yet after checking with staff and patients, they discovered his form to be a ghost.

Recently, nurses have been getting so concerned about his visitations that Father Vin Whelan, a Roman Catholic priest from Our Lady's was called in *twice* within the 1991/2 period, and blessed the ward by praying, and sprinkling holy water.

St Thomas's hospital has always been the subject of ghostly speculation, and I myself have heard tales from a variety of sources including nurses and a member of my family who once attended as an out-patient. Unfortunately, these stories are always quite vague and no thorough investigation has ever taken place to gather all the information together.

Ghosts of Gawsworth

Gawsworth Hall must be the most widely haunted area in Cheshire, for well documented accounts come not only from the Hall, but from the nearby churchyard, the Old Rectory, the lanes thereabouts, the Harrington Arms public house, and Maggoty's Wood nearby. Although the activity is scattered, it does not diminish in force or interest, providing a whole range of stories and legends which only enhance the romantic atmosphere of the beautiful Hall, and its idyllic surroundings.

The site of Gawsworth Hall has housed families for over nine

43

hundred years, so it is hardly surprising that some of its residents have lingered on for a while longer! The stories begin really with the most famous resident of Gawsworth, Mary Fitton. At one time it was claimed that she may have been the "Dark Lady" of Shakespeare's sonnets, but that is highly debatable nowadays. From this connection, she also attained quite a reputation as a seductress, although this too, is now debatable. Introduced to the Royal Court of Queen Elizabeth when she was just seventeen, she was soon noted by the gentlemen for her beauty and lively personality. Certainly, around the turn of the century, she became mistress to the Earl of Pembroke, and within a year it was discovered that she was to bear his child. Such scandal did not look good for the Royal Court, and Pembroke was sent to Fleet Prison (after having refused to marry Mary), and Mary herself was sacked from Court.

Gawsworth: the Old Rectory

44

That was not the end of her problems however, when she returned home to Gawsworth she was banished from the family Hall (for the dishonour she brought them) and lived in the Old Rectory. To further her troubles, the son she was carrying died soon after birth. Rumours of other affairs abounded, but not much is certain. In 1607 she married Captain Polwhele after having already bore him a child. She died in 1647, leaving the name of Lougher, having been married again to an Irish Captain. So much effort has been made to establish how many men she had affairs with, that her personal problems and children have been totally forgotten. This is very sad, and seems to be emphasised by Mary herself, who is one of the more reliable ghosts at Gawsworth, after having such a troubled life.

Her ghost has been seen many times around the grounds of the Hall, possibly in the churchyard, the Old Rectory and the Harrington Arms, but not as much evidence is present to support these. However what is more well known, by local farmers especially, is the fact that she walks down the lane from the Old Rectory to the Harrington Arms, usually by the side of a lone young man.

A friend of mine, Mr. Sam Bailey, had heard tales of this happening, but never believed them until one lonely Autumn night when he was taking a short cut down the lane to meet some friends in the pub. The journey was uneventful until he reached the Old Rectory, when he suddenly felt extremely cold and frightened, and was aware that someone was walking with him on his left-hand side. This was where the cold came from, but he was unable to fully turn around to look. What he saw out of the corner of his eye was enough! By his side was a woman, walking at the same pace, and dressed in old fashioned long green dress. Sam was so frightened in this darkened lane, all alone with just a ghostly lady for company, that he could not find the strength to run, just to quicken his pace a little, all the time trying to close the distance to the now very appealing pub at the end of the lane. She kept pace with him, also walking a little faster. In this fashion, the two of them journeyed together to the crossroads just outside the Harrington Arms. As soon as the lane ended and the pub came into sight "She just disappeared", he said. The freezing cold along his left side went with her, but gave way to shock, and he was probably the most enthusiastic customer of the pub that night! His friends were concerned by his shivering on such a mild night, which is hardly surprising because he described the chill from the ghost as "unnatural", "deep", and that it "went straight to the bone". This tallies with many descriptions of "cold spots" in other cases.

The lane at Gawsworth, where the ghostly apparition was seen.

After having related his story, he was later shown portraits of Mary Fitton, whom it was presumed the ghost was, and he said they definitely bore some resemblance, but that this lady was more "casual, with her hair loose around her shoulders".

Another well-attested account comes from a worker at the Hall, who was travelling home by car late one morning, around 2am. When he approached the church area, probably just turning into the aforementioned lane, he saw who he thought was the owner of the Hall, Mrs. Monica Richards. He waved to her, but received no response. Instead, she started to cross the road right in front of his car, forcing him to make an emergency stop. Concerned, he got out of the car to see if she was all right, but could find no sign that anyone had been there. It was later verified that Mrs. Richards certainly wasn't there at that time.

Mary Fitton's ghost is not just confined to dark lanes though! She has been seen in the churchyard, and was well-known to haunt the Old Rectory, as Sam Bailey, a long-term resident of the area, told me. He said that the Rectory was well-known for its annoying poltergeist disturbances, and the vague apparition of a man.

The Hall itself has had its share of supernatural visitations. One confusing habit of the ghost there is to produce a psychic odour, which in this case is incense. In February 1971, Monica Richards suddenly smelt incense in her bedroom, although she had no idea where it could have come from. One clue may be that the room was situated directly below the Priest's Room, which also suffers from the strange odour. On other occasions the psychic odour has been known to precede the visit of an Archbishop. On one such visit the Archbishop thanked the Richards for being so considerate, by burning incense. They were completely taken aback, as they thought the churchman had brought it along himself!

Other ghostly goings-on in the Hall include poltergeist activity, things moving around and breaking without explanation, bangs and raps emanating from empty rooms, and a disembodied female voice. More startling though was an account Mrs. Richards related to me when I visited the Hall one Sunday afternoon. Several years ago, she was upstairs in a private room when she heard what she thought was a late visitor to the Hall. She came down the stairs to see if he needed any help, and was shocked to see the ghostly form of a man stood on the staircase near an alcove. He seemed to turn towards her, and she described him as very dark, especially around the eyes, and that he had a little pointed beard. As she moved closer, he seemed to step back into the alcove, and she felt a sharp pain in her chest. Then he just disappeared. There was no trace that anyone had ever been there. She did not feel frightened or threatened by the man, and is rather disappointed that she has not seen him again.

Perhaps a clue to at least some of the activity is a discovery made in 1921 in the Oratory, which is next to the Priest's Room. A full human skeleton was uncovered, and given a proper burial in the churchyard, but no one was ever able to identify the bones. The only suggestion was that perhaps (as happened in many places) it was the body of a priest hidden during the Reformation, though this is pure conjecture.

By far the most light-hearted, and certainly my favourite ghost of Gawsworth is that of the Eighteenth Century playwright and dancing-master, Samuel "Maggoty" Johnson. As the last real court jester in England, "Maggoty" was widely regarded as an eccentric, (incidentally, the nickname applied is actually an old phrase meaning that the person "has maggots in their brain", or is a little odd). He was paid to entertain the guests in Gawsworth, and to play the fool. This he did so well, that he was also in demand from other stately homes in the area, including Lyme. Considering his reputation, it is hardly surprising that even his attitude to death and the afterlife, would be light-hearted. His last wish was to buried in unconsecrated ground, challenging the upheld belief that souls buried without a religious service, would return as ghosts. This certainly seems to have proved correct, because the ghostly shape of a man in tight trousers and cockscomb with bells, has been seen several times in Maggoty's Wood. This tends to happen close to his grave, which has a special inscription to relate his rather odd choice to anyone who wishes to see it.

Opposite: Maggoty Johnson's ghost

48

'Maggoty' Johnson.

M.G.Mills © 1994

Sam again told us that on one particular occasion, the wood had an even covering of snow, and one witness saw the dancing form of the jolly man, at first believing it to be a stranger, perhaps having sampled too much of the local brew! But as the witness approached the spot where the figure had been enjoying himself, the most striking fact was that there were no footprints in the snow! As far as the ground covering was concerned, that was the first person to walk in the wood since the snowfall.

Maggoty Johnson's grave

Considering this tale, it also interesting to note the experience once again of Sam Bailey, who used to live in the area.

He was returning home very late one night, along the road which runs directly parallel to Maggoty's Wood. Driving along, he approached a crossroads (which encompasses the corner of the wood) and was shocked to see a dark shape stood in the middle of the road. It appeared all of a sudden "just out of nowhere" he said, and as a consequence he couldn't stop the car in time to avoid hitting it. As the car ploughed into the shape, Sam said "the whole windscreen just turned black, like there was a sheet over it. I couldn't see anything". He finally came to a stop, and jumped out of the car to see what he had hit, although he admitted feeling "nervous, because I didn't think I'd hit anything, well, natural, if you know what I mean". His suspicions were well founded, because although he left the car the instant it stopped, there was nothing to be seen in any direction along the crossroads, not even an animal running away. He didn't wait around " to see it come back", but hurried off in his car feeling extremely frightened in the dark country lanes.

This experience occurred just outside Maggoty's Wood, which has been considerably shortened since the jester's day, to accommodate new housing. Although it is by no means definite, it would seem sensible to suggest that Sam actually ran over the long dead Maggoty Johnson.

This closes the account of the ghosts of Gawsworth, but it is definitely the place to go for would-be ghosthunters! Even if you don't experience anything, the place is well worth a visit for its historical interest and general beauty.

3

Cheshire Folklore

Cheshire's Mythological Residents

As with most counties, Cheshire is steeped in folkloric beliefs, and still contains many legends and tales inspired by our pagan ancestors. Perhaps the most glamorous of these legends, is that of the mermaid.

Rostherne Mere claims the existence not only of the ghostly bell mentioned in chapter one, but also of a beautiful maiden who appears on Easter Sunday to ring the said bell. She is said to rise gracefully out of the water and sing a melodic song which makes witnesses feel peaceful and happy. Unfortunately, no single witness can be identified, but the legend still remains.

A second mermaid is said to grace the waters near Leasowe Castle (itself curiously the subject of a ghost story as well). She is said to be seen and heard singing on bright moonlit nights, although the exact location is rather sketchy. T.A. Coward in his 1932 book "Cheshire", said she had been seen "attending her toilet in the somewhat unabashed manner of more modern maidens" and that she was "fatally fascinating to susceptible youths"

To reinforce Cheshire's connection with mermaids, an Eighteenth Century popular story told of one such sea nymph near Liverpool, in a place called Black Rock. The story follows the more well-known legend that mermaids boded death for sailors, who were frequently dragged to the murky depths of the sea by beautiful women.

Opposite: the mermaid myth

52

M.G.Mills
©1994

This tale was more romantic though, telling of a sailor, John Robinson, who took a mermaid aboard his ship and kept her there for quite a while. When she left, she gave him a ring as a token of affection but, true to legend, he died just five days later in the supposed safety of his own home.

Dragons

From the subtle foreboding of mermaids, I move on to the much more blatant and entertaining legend of dragons. Indeed, Cheshire holds claim to its own St George, under the name of Thomas Venables. It is said that during the reign of Henry VI, a dragon began terrorising the people of Moston, doing such terrible things as eating babies and young maidens. Apparently, the creature "devoured all such persons that he laid hold on." Several brave men attempted to slay the beast, but had all failed, and suffered an agonising death. There is no description of this dragon, but according to legends it could vary from a large worm-shaped animal, to the caricatured fairy-tale style, fire breathing, bescaled monster. Whichever type Thomas Venables encountered, he did so "valiantly and courageously", attacking the monster with his arrows. The first arrow hit the dragon in the eye, but didn't kill it, so Venables used other weapons and "manfullie slew him, at which instant the dragon was devouringe of a childe".

This tale of bravery was well received, and the Venables crest actually depicts the triumph, as it shows a dragon with an arrow in its eye, murdering a child. Middlewich church is supposed to possess a carved screen with the crest upon it. The village of Moston also named Dragon's Lake after the event.

Opposite: Thomas Venables and the dragon

M.G.Mills
© 1994

Giant tales

Even more fantastic is the presence of giants in Cheshire's legends. It is said that a castle once stood on the site of Arden Hall, which was home to a giant. This giant occupied himself by throwing large stones at another giant who lived in Stockport! What the local people thought about this is not recorded, but it seems that no one was crushed in this fairytale-like battle. After becoming impatient with a long arduous fight, the Arden giant hoarded all his rocks and threw them furiously at his rival, who was so overcome that he had to admit defeat.

Several visits by the Devil himself have been recorded in old Cheshire's history. One such visit saw the Devil beaten at his own game by a Friar named Francis. Apparently, the Devil flew over Vale Royal one night, saw the Friar asleep, and thought him fair game. He said to the holy man

"Oh, Friar, of ale thou shalt wassail thy fill
If I may be witness to thy last will,
And all the fat bucks in broad Cheshire are thine
If here on this parchment thy name thou wilt sign."

The Friar, realising that his soul was in danger, agreed to the terms laid out, but only if he could make a condition of his own, which he would reveal after he had signed the agreement. The Devil, confident of his own infallibility, hastily agreed to this. The paper was duly signed, and the Friar told the Devil of his extra condition, which was "that on yonder sands of Merton you shall twine me a dozen hay-bands". Pleased with his apparent success, the Devil left to fulfil this simple chore, only to find that there was no grass long enough on Merton sands, as it was widely known to be barren. The Friar had won the bargain, but just to make sure his soul was never in danger, the local residents ploughed the land every year thereafter and never planted upon it.

The monks of Vale Royal had another encounter with the Devil, but this time it was a harder battle. It involved a church in the village of Over, which the Devil had taken a particular dislike to. So much so that one day he lifted the church from its foundations in the centre of the village, and began flying off with it! What his diabolical aim was, no one knows, but the monks in Vale Royal immediately began praying and cursing, to stop and fight the Devil. This seemed to have no effect until the Abbey bells sounded long and loud. Hearing this holy music, the Devil dropped the church, much to the monks' horror, who feared the building would be destroyed. To protect it during its fall, they prayed to St Chad, to whom the church is dedicated, who answered by cushioning the fall. The church landed a mile away from its original location, where it still stands today.

Cheshire's Legendary Visitors

Cheshire claims a connection with Robin Hood, who is supposed to have visited the county. In Tilston Fearnall there is reputed to be a barrow named "Robin Hood's Barrow", upon which the archer stood to fire an arrow at Beeston Crag. His visit must have been more than just a passing through because there are other locations which claim an association with him.

It is said that Robin Hood stood on Werneth Low and threw a rock at the Cheshire Plain. The stone fell in the River Tame and is supposed to still show the handprint, the fingers having indented themselves in the stone!

The third and last place Robin visited in Cheshire is Ludworth Moor, near Marple Bridge which boasts two large standing stones which he apparently used for target practice.

Another famous, or infamous visitor to old Cheshire was the notorious highwayman Dick Turpin. Passing through the area, he robbed and murdered a lawyer, when he was in Newbridge Hollow near Altrincham. Turpin then supposedly rode like the wind to Hoo Green, where he stopped outside an inn called the "Kilton". He struck a man hard with his whip, and demanded to know the time.

He was later arrested for the crime, but the man at the inn was able to testify in his defence, recounting his experience, and remembering the exact time. The court reached the decision that it

57

was impossible for anyone to ride from Newbridge Hollow to Hoo Green in such a short time, and therefore Turpin could not have committed the murder.

Cheshire did boast its own variation of Turpin, this being Edward Higgins, a gentleman of the county who spent his time wining and dining with the local nobility, and was widely respected. But there was a darker side to his nature, because after his guests had left, he would ride out in the garb of a highwayman, and rob their coaches! His activities did not stop on the road though, as he became more daring, he would break into their houses and help himself to jewels boasted of just hours before at his own home in Knutsford!

He was reported to have stolen a snuff box belonging to a Mr. Egerton who had been entertaining Higgins, and when at a house in Chester, he broke into a lady's bedroom and began rifling through her jewellery box. To his surprise though, she was not fully asleep, and having heard him moving about, called out "Oh Mary! You know how tired I am, can't you put the things straight in the morning?" At his trial, Higgin's said that if the lady hadn't mistaken him for her maid, then he would have murdered her there and then. Another close call for Higgins was when he decided to follow Lady Warburton's coach after a party, to relieve her of her jewels disguised as a common highwayman. His outfit couldn't have been very convincing though, because as he rode up to stop the coach, Lady Warburton leaned out of the window and said "Goodnight, Mr. Higgins! Why did you leave the ball so early?" This dual life ended abruptly though when he was arrested for housebreaking in Wales, and eventually executed at Carmarthen, leaving a considerable amount of egg on the faces of the nobility who had sworn by his honest reputation.

Right: Higgins, the highwayman

M.S. MILLS
1994

Alderley Edge and the Merlin Legend

An article in the Manchester Mail of 1805 described an encounter which was already many years old. Thomas Broadhurst related the story of a Mobberley farmer who actually met the famous wizard – Merlin. The story goes that the man had bred a beautiful white horse, and was taking her to Macclesfield to sell, expecting a very good price. When he got to the area named Thieves' Hole, he was rather shocked to see a man appear nearby, as if out of nowhere. The man was old, very tall, and was wearing a long, dress-type outfit, which looked very strange. He stopped the farmer and offered to buy the horse. The farmer refused, thinking he could probably get a better deal in Macclesfield. The old man seemed rather angry, and declared that the farmer would not be *able* to sell the horse, and that on his way back through the wood, they would meet again. The farmer scoffed at such a notion, but was shocked when the old man's prophecy came true.

Later that day he was indeed walking back through the Edge, feeling disappointed that lots of people had shown an interest in his beautiful horse, but no one wished to buy it. Sure enough, he met the old man again, who simply said, "follow me". This he did silently, past the Seven Firs, Golden Stone, Stormy Point and Saddle Boll, until the farmer thought he could hear a horse neighing below his feet! Suddenly the old man produced what looked like a magic wand, with which he touched a large rock directly in front of them. The farmer watched in amazement as two large iron gates appeared in place of the rock. They opened slowly and loudly, the horse panicking and throwing the man to the floor. Seeing how frightened the farmer was, the old man told him he had nothing to fear and said he was about to "behold a sight which no mortal eye has ever looked upon".

As they went inside the cave, the farmer realised that this was where he had heard the horse neighing from, because it opened out into a big cavern, and there in front of him lay countless white horses just like his own, and an army of men in old-fashioned clothes. Speechless, he continued following the old man who led him to a large pile of gold coins and treasure. He was told to take payment for his horse from there, as the army was short of one white horse, and would one day rise again when they were needed to save England. This, the man said would be when George, the son of George reigns. Another account says that the men were actually King Arthur and his knights, and the old man was Merlin, the famous magician.

The farmer was then told to leave, but that no one else would ever see the iron gates or cave again. This, if nothing else, appears to be true.

The wizard figure is certainly remembered at Alderley, although

Merlin remembered: at The Wizard restaurant

62

whether it is Merlin or not, is debatable. The Wizard Inn reflects the tradition, as does the Wizard's Well which bears the inscription

"Drink of this and take thy fill
For the water falls by the wizard's will!"

A figure has been seen around the Edge, which several people claimed to be Merlin, although it was much more likely to have been Alex Saunders, self-proclaimed "King of the Witches" in his ritual robes, who used to visit the atmospheric spot frequently. The area is still noted today for its supernatural qualities, and actually has to be cordoned off on the night of Hallowe'en because of the hundreds of people that gather there on this spooky night!

Cures and Customs

Cheshire's old customs and beliefs make little sense to us now in the days of modern medicine and practical thinking, but there was a time when any bad luck was caused by demons and strange precautions had to be taken against any illness, bad spirits, or just your fate in years to come.

Many of the beliefs surrounded the farmsteads, and countless warnings and advise were at hand for the farmer interested in folklore. For example, the farrowing of the sow could be aided by feeding her a large piece of toast spread with plenty of lard, which supposedly stopped the pig from eating her own offspring. When the farmer's wife was making bread, she also had to beware of evil spirits who would stop the dough from rising! This she guarded against by making the sign of the cross over the mixing bowl.

Many strange cures for ailments were used, for example, rubbing a wart with a piece of meat, and then burying the meat, with the understanding that as the meat decayed and faded away, so would the wart. Burying things and associating them with illness or bad luck, was a common belief, as if the object actually took on the characteristics of the disease, freeing the sufferer completely. Other strange remedies included sewing the shoulder bone of a rabbit in up in a cloth and carrying it around as a cure for rheumatism; and cutting a live toad in half, burying one half and carrying the other around as a cure for scrofula, a kind of tuberculosis known as the King's evil.

Parents of a child with whooping cough could use the "split-tree" cure. This involved finding a briar bush with an arched branch, and passing the child underneath it. Carrying a raw potato around with you every day was believed to prevent the onset of rheumatism. Fletcher Moss said in 1895 that "a fine, fat spider, all alive and kicking" was a good cure for ague and many other illnesses. Spider's webs were also used as an aid to stop bleeding, and snails and young frogs as a cure for consumption. Dropsy could be cured by taking a dose of powdered cockroaches, and woodlice were eaten as tablets for a range of illnesses. If you suffered from earache, you were advised to roast an onion and put it up against your ear for some time. People who had trouble sleeping, or disturbed sleep were obliged to eat roasted mice or mouse pie! For a bad cough, live frogs were to be held to the mouth, and one lady reported that "her lad's cough would not go, though he'd sucked two toads to death!" Many of these strange cures were still in use in 1895, although mainly by country people.

Many illnesses were thought to have been brought on by witches' spells rather than communicated from an infected person, or slowly developing over a number of years. As a consequence it was also important to guard against witches, and to deflect any spells directed at an individual. Fletcher Moss remembered as a child having to throw any frogs or toads found in the house, into the fire, as they were thought to be witches in disguise. It was said that if the root of your fingernail became torn and painful, you had a "stepmother's blessing", which was a mild bewitching.

As you can see, these cures involved either killing, or using parts of dead animals, but it did not end there. Even more potent as cures were parts of a human corpse. There are actually accounts of riots at the gallows, by crowds anxious for parts of the dead body to cure themselves, and loved ones from such things as skin complaints, scrofula, ulcers, tumours and cancers. Here we find the meaning of the phrase "the blood is the life". Skulls and teeth were especially endowed with healing power, the teeth also being used as replacements for rotten ones in the general public's mouths. Toothache could be cured by wearing a tooth found in a churchyard around your neck, and if this didn't work, then the offending tooth would be extracted, and the "new" one put in.

The right hand of a hanged or gibbeted criminal was also greatly sought after. It was thought to have amazing powers when transformed into a "Hand of Glory". This affectionate term was misleading because the severed hand would be dried out thoroughly, and then a special mixture containing the fat of a hanged man, virgin wax, and Lapland Sesame (thought to be dried horse manure to make the mixture burn easily!), was prepared and formed into candles. Then, either a single candle was placed in the palm, or several wedged between the fingers before the instrument was used under cover of darkness to rob houses. The perpetrator would hold the Hand of Glory up outside a particular house they wished to rob, and recite the following rhyme

"Let those who rest more deeply sleep,
While those awake their vigils keep.
O Hand of Glory shed thy light,
Guide us to our spoil tonight!"

This was supposed to magically open all locked doors, and let sleepers fall into a kind of trance so they would not wake up, and if anyone was still awake, one flash of the hand and they would instantly be struck motionless and speechless, and lose all memory of the burglars. The only thing that could stop the Hand of Glory's effects was to extinguish the flames with milk. Whether it actually worked is not known, but was certainly used widely around Britain. One is on display in Whitby's museum, and an attempted burglary using the device was foiled in 1797 in Cumbria.

Many superstitions surrounded weddings and funerals, the most important being that the two groups never met. This custom was especially important at Barthomley where each group always used a different entrance, the right hand for funerals, and the left for weddings. If one of the marrying couple passed through the gates at the funeral entrance, it was believed that death would strike the couple within their first year of marriage. The bride's pathway to the church and the threshold of her home would be "sanded" to bring her good luck in her forthcoming marriage, in some districts.

It was thought in some places that houses in which a death occurred were cursed and had to be closed up for a certain period of time. Ironically, it was also believed that any house which remained empty for a number of years would become inhabited by evil spirits and demons. This shows how customs varied from district to district, and the ignorance surrounding death and the afterlife only served to reinforce the speculation, and encouraged the formation of strange ideas to protect the living from the dead.

This fear of death prompted interest in shrines and sacred life-giving waters. Such a well was situated in Delamere Forest, where a holy spring was said to cure the blind, deaf and arthritic. Spurstow also boasted a well with curative powers, which was widely used in the Eighteenth Century. Spurstow White Water provided healing baths for lame people, who left their crutches by the well as a memorial. The water apparently smelled of sulphuretted hydrogen, leading T.A. Coward in his 1932 book "Cheshire" to conclude that "it is probable that it really was useful". According to old accounts there was a signpost to Spurstow with the verses

"If you are troubled with sore or flaw,
This is the way to Spurstow Spa."

And pointing away from Spurstow, it said

"If all your sores you've left in the lurch,
This is the way to Bunbury Church."

Such wells and shrines were often dedicated to different gods, and sacrifices left for a person's wish to be granted. Although none are recorded in Cheshire, it was occasionally the case that a human sacrifice was used.

Another religious curiosity is said to stand in the grounds of Chester Cathedral. Apparently, part of the famous Glastonbury Thorn grows there, and flowers every Christmas. the legend goes that Joseph of Arimathea came over to Britain and rested on what is now Glastonbury. When he woke up he was surprised to see his faithful staff, which he had carried through many countries had taken root in the ground, and had begun to flower. This showed him that his travels were over, and he could rest. Quite how the legend has filtered through to Chester though, is not clear.

Crossroads and Corpses

Crossroads have long been known as uncanny and supernatural places, perhaps because of the crossing of paths and the choices it presents; if the wrong choice is made it could bring bad luck and danger, just as in all life's decisions, with everyone fearing the thought of getting lost. As with many things in the past that people were afraid of, it was rationalised by the allocation of a god or goddess, who could control the fates of people who either pleased or displeased them. For this reason, Hecate was seen to be the goddess of the crossroads, as she had three faces all looking in different directions, and was seen to represent the different phases of our personalities and development. To gain her goodwill, cakes and gifts were often left at crossroads where her followers, ghosts and restless spirits, were said to gather.

For this reason, suicides and murderers were often buried at crossroads because it was *expected* that they would return as ghosts. The idea was that if the ghost did rise, it would not know where it was, or what path to take to return to the village and haunt the occupants. Throughout the country many different methods were used to prevent the ghost or vampire (at one time they were seen as the same thing) attacking the living. Usually though, the body was taken to an allotted crossroads under the cover of darkness, and was not allowed a Christian burial. In the case of suicides this was because they were seen to have committed "self-murder" ("Felo-de-se"). A wooden stake then had to be cut, and unceremoniously hammered into the heart of the corpse.

One variation used in Cheadle was to tie the body to a stake at the bottom of the grave, again to prevent the ghost from "escaping".

The entrance to Stockport museum, a popular spot for a crossroad burial.

Henry Heginbothom, the Stockport historian also related how a crossroads near to the Vernon Park Museum was a favourite spot for these activities, and skeletons have actually been discovered there, with stakes through their hearts!

Luckily, the Law which decreed these uncouth burials was abolished in 1823, but suicides were still banished to remote parts of the churchyard. The suspicions linking suicides and ghosts/vampires obviously still existed in 1832 as one man, Samuel Tongue, was buried at midnight in St Thomas's churchyard in Stockport.

Criminals and witches were occasionally executed at crossroads, again so that their vengeful spirits would not be able to find their way home. Gibbets were also hung there, but it was probably so that more people would see the felon, and be deterred from crime when it was gruesomely displayed in such a lonely and eerie place.

St Thomas' churchyard, where Samuel Tongue was buried at midnight

Due to the supernatural associations given to crossroads, it is not surprising that they soon became known as witches' meeting places, and a prime place to contact the Devil, and perform black magic. It is said that during the Seventeenth Century, witches regularly danced at crossroads to summon the Devil.

With the advent of motor cars and street lighting etc., these practices have ceased because the places have lost their dark and eerie atmosphere.

Smuggling, Wrecking and Sea Folklore

In the early Nineteenth Century, Cheshire ranked along with Cornwall as one of the worst places in the country for wrecking and smuggling. It centred mainly around the Wirral area which was extremely desolate and rarely frequented by the local constabulary. Surrounded by marshes and bogs, it was inhabited by just a few hardy residents who had plenty of opportunity to lure ships laden with expensive cargo, to a watery end on the rocky coastline. They would shine lights to guide the captains into what was supposedly a safe harbour during bad weather and fog. The locals would then avidly grab the strewn cargo, and either sell it or keep it for themselves. The police were rumoured to have been in league with them, as they never took much action against the cruel crime. It was even said that the people robbed the dead or drowning sailors and then killed those who lived, to keep their ghastly crime secret.

One tale, probably invented to aid the smugglers in their secret work, was of a bridge near Prenton on the Wirral. It was supposedly made from a whale's jawbone with crossbeams added to it, and if anyone dared cross it at night, the legend goes that they would be brutally murdered by the ghosts of two drowned sailors who guarded the bridge.

As I said before, smuggling flourished along the Wirral and the Mersey estuary. This was aided by the convenient location of Mother Redcap's Inn, which was a notorious meeting place for smugglers, and storehouse for contraband. It was apparently named after a woman, Poll Jones, who always wore a red hood, although there are variations on this. The Inn itself was extremely isolated, and under cover of darkness the boats filled with illegal imports would follow the incoming tide, which led them virtually up to the door of the tavern, and the wares would be hidden in the cellar. On one occasion, a ship laden with silks and other material was looted and stored in Mother Redcap's cellar, and consequently next summer all the women in Seascomb, Wallasey, Liscard and Bidston wore silk dresses of the same material and design! As an extra precaution, the inn boasted a false weather vane, and if it pointed inland everything was fine, but if it pointed out towards the Mersey then it acted as a warning to the smugglers that the Revenue men were on the alert, and consequently they stayed away until the all clear was given.

Moving inland for a moment, Northwich was a successful salt mining town in the last century, which also attracted smugglers because the commodity was taxed. To escape this large reduction in their profits, some of the townsfolk hit on an idea to transport the salt away from Northwich without the tax-man ever seeing it. As one of the men was an undertaker, the salt was packed away in coffins and slowly driven through the town with a convincing string of mourners. This scheme worked well for a while, but the procession always had to go past the Town Hall, whose officials became alarmed at the large number of deaths in their town over such a short period of time. Eventually this suspicion led to an investigation, and salt was discovered in the coffins.

The sea was the main route for contraband in Cheshire though, but the dangers were high with old ships, bad lighting, and the terrible rocky coastline. These risks obviously resulted in many deaths, prompting belief in strange superstitions to gain even the smallest amount of good luck or protection. One such precaution was for sailors to obtain a dried caul from a newly born baby, and carry this with him to protect him from shipwreck and drowning.

The sea itself was seen as a living entity which could claim the lives of those persons it took a dislike to. But this worked the opposite way around for the River Dee. This was once named the "Holy Dee", as it was worshipped for having special powers. Among these was the fact that if any Christian person drowned in its waters, a mysterious light would appear over the corpse, enabling it to be located and retrieved for a proper Christian burial.

Much superstition was also attached to drowned and drowning people, because it was thought that once the sea had claimed a soul, nothing should interfere with that, forcing most corpses to be buried below the tide line, or just thrown back. In some cases it was even thought that to rescue a drowning individual, would only make the sea claim the soul of someone else for compensation, usually the person who had embarked upon the rescue. So it was not unknown for people to stand by and watch a drowning, without lifting a finger to help!

However, along parts of the old Cheshire coastline, it was believed that if a drowned corpse washed up along the shore, whoever found it must give it a Christian burial, or else the ghost of the poor soul would come back and haunt the finder for the rest of his life.

Miscellaneous Curiosities

A man from Handley near Tattenhall named Mr. Allen became distraught when he was unable to marry the woman he loved, because both his and her parents objected viciously and forbade the match. As a consequence, it is said that he sold everything he owned and lived as a hermit in a cave, so disenchanted was he with the human race. He lived in his cave on Bickerton Hill for the rest of his life, (he was reported to still have been alive and well at the grand age of ninety-nine). The cave is now known for this legend, and referred to as Mad Allen's Hole because the man supposedly went insane in his isolation and loneliness, wishing he could marry the woman he loved.

A rather comical legend is connected to the Roodee Race-course, just outside the city walls of Chester. It is said that as long ago as the Tenth Century Lady Trawst, wife of the Governor of Hawarden went to a statue of Our Lady to pray for rain in the midst of a terrible drought. Luckily, as soon as she had finished praying, a thunderstorm boomed loudly and rain began to fall. It seemed as if a miracle had occurred until the statue was struck by lightning, and fell on the poor woman, killing her instantly. So respected was she among the local people that the statue was actually put on trial for murder! It was found guilty, and sentenced to death by hanging. However, this was somewhat difficult, and the alternative of burning was not suitable for a holy statue, so a compromise was reached – that of drowning. The statue was duly tied to a cross, and left on the banks of the River Dee whose tide carried it to the centre of Chester, where it was found and reverently carried to St John's Church.

During the Reformation it was said that such a statue was in St John's, but it was converted to a whipping block for students who misbehaved, because it was a Catholic idol. Eventually it was set on fire and consequently disposed of. There are several variations on this legend, including a version where the statue was "drowned", because the rain did not come despite the prayers of the locals. T.A. Coward in "Cheshire" repeated a rather damning rhyme, which the residents of Chester wrote when they rescued the statue.

"The Jews their God did crucify,
The Hardeners theirs did drown:
'Cause with their wants she'd not comply
And lies under this cold stone."

* * *

Around the early Fifteenth Century, at the time when Cheshire men were constantly at war with the Welsh over the borders of the River Dee, the Mayor of Chester banned Welshmen from the streets of his City after sunset, and during the day permitted them only to carry a knife to cut their food, and no other weapon. This was an improvement, however from the Fourteenth Century, when any Welshman in the city after sunset risked being beheaded! These regulations resulted in much resentment and ill-feeling by individuals, and ultimately the Mayor's death.

During the Chester Fair one year a Welshman, Reinallt, found himself in a heated and violent argument because of his nationality. Feeling as if he had been unjustly treated, and seeking revenge, he grabbed the Mayor and rushed off with him, back to his castle in Mold, Clwyd. Always in front of the band of soldiers pursuing him, he hung the Mayor from the battlements at the castle, and left with his own soldiers. Soon enough, up to two hundred soldiers from Chester reached the castle and forced their way in. Once

73

inside, they discovered the dead body of the Mayor. Too late, they realised it was a trap as Reinallt's men closed the gates behind them and set fire to the whole castle, killing most of the soldiers. Those who did escape the blaze were brutally slaughtered by the waiting men outside the gates. It is hardly surprising that the feud with Wales continued for many years afterwards.

* * *

John Turner lived in a small village called Saltersford near Rainow, and made his living by transporting goods with his pack-hoses between Chester and Derby.

On Christmas Eve, 1735, there was a particularly vicious snowstorm, and he was advised not to attempt the dangerous journey home. But with it being such a special occasion, he was anxious to be at home with his family, at least for Christmas Day, and went ahead despite the terrible conditions. He never reached his home, and the family spent Christmas Day awaiting his return. When he didn't arrive, a search party was sent out, and found his frozen body just a mile away from Saltersford. As if the shock weren't enough, in the fresh snow there was the mark of a woman's single footprint by the lone corpse. It was never discovered where it had come from, and why there was just one print. Rumours abounded that a ghostly herald had ushered John Turner from his icy grave to another, warmer, life after death.

* * *

An old woman from Lymm was criticised for being "blasphemous" when she continually refused to walk to the village pump for her water, but preferred to take a bucket to the church downspout, and fill it from there.

She was warned many times by her neighbours that she would be punished by God for such actions, but she continued to ignore them. However, one day, as she was filling her bucket from the spout, a skeleton hand protruded from the pipe, hit her on the head, pinched the bucket, and disappeared back up it again, leaving the woman stunned and rather frightened by this "divine

Lymm church: site for a skeletal hand

warning"! She was reluctant to tell her neighbours of the true cause for alarm, and told them that she had been struck by lightning, but she never returned to the spot again, preferring to walk the distance to the pump, than encounter the skeleton hand again!

* * *

The well at Beeston Castle had a profound impression on a servant from the castle many years ago. At three hundred and sixty six feet in depth, it was no mean feat for someone in those days to reach the bottom. Tales abounded of buried treasure, and a volunteer was needed to search for it. The young man was carefully lowered down whilst everyone at the top waited with bated breath for his findings. However, when he was raised up again he had lost the power of speech and gone mad. No one could find out exactly *what* he had encountered down there, and the poor man died soon after. It certainly deterred any other would-be treasure hunters from taking the journey down such a dark and mysterious well. As time passed though, people began to doubt the authenticity of the rumours, and another trip was made to the bottom. This time, nothing was encountered, and the only treasure found was a fox's skull.

* * *

Mrs Mary Davies of Great Saughall near Chester became famous at the end of the Seventeenth Century because she actually had horns growing on her head! The phenomena began before she was thirty years old, after a strange growth appeared and began to resemble horns. Four years later, these horns fell off, and another set grew! This actually happened two or three more times, making her case famous, and well observed. The Ashmolean Museum in Oxford has a portrait of her, and also one of the original horns. She did not mind the publicity about her deformity and was able to live comfortably on the income from that alone. Despite her material well-being though, the horns were said to give her quite a bit of pain, "especially upon the change of the weather." As with many curiosities, T. A. Coward printed a rhyme about her in his book "Picturesque Cheshire", published in 1903:

"You that love wonders to behold,
Here you may of a wonder read
The strangest that was ever seen or told,
A woman with horns upon her head."

She was said to have regularly shown her horns off "at the sign of the Swan near Charring Cross", until she died at the age of seventy.

* * *

Another subject that attracted much attention, and the opportunity to make some money (as indeed it still does today) was that of engineering a romance, or finding out who was to be your husband/wife in the future.

One scheme used in Cheshire was mentioned in Fletcher Moss' 1898 book "Folklore, Old customs and Tales of my Neighbours". He related how a man from Gatley desperately wanted a certain woman to fall in love with him. All his efforts at wooing her had failed, and he turned to alternative methods. Following the local folklore, he bought a dried placenta, costing him two guineas from a local witch, and buried it at the threshold of the lady's home. This method was widely believed to work, but lady in question was so strong willed that it had no effect.

For a lady, the "wishing steps" along the Chester Walls would have to suffice. If she could run up and down the sixty or seventy steps without taking a breath, and make a wish (that of who she wanted to marry), then her dream would supposedly come true.

At the opposite end of the scale, it was also possible for men to sell their wives if they were unhappy with them! This happened in Stockport outside the White Lion public house in 1851. Mr. William Clayton held his wife up for auction, eventually receiving five shillings for her from a Mr. J. Booth. If at any time the wife (unnamed) had objected to the proceedings, she was carefully controlled by the use of a halter (an iron band with a chain fixed to it to lead the prisoner) around her neck.

The place to auction your wife: The White Lion in Stockport

Altrincham Market Place was also the scene of such an auction, when a "Mobberley worthy" had his wife led in, also with a halter around her neck. However, she must have objected more strongly, as a friend was required to stand behind her with a thick stick to persuade her to continue! The lady was subject to further embarrassment though, as the bidding was so slow that one shilling and sixpence was eventually accepted – a grand total of seven and a half pence in today's currency!

* * *

Changing the subject now, a row of Spanish Chestnut trees between Toft and Ollerton, were at the centre of a curse in the last century. The tale, similar to one told of Dunham Park, goes that the squire of a neighbouring Hall was anxious for the birth of a son, to inherit the Hall and the family name. However, each child to be born turned out to be a girl, greatly enraging the father, who planted a tree for each girl as her inheritance, and impatiently awaited the next birth which would hopefully be a boy. Seven girls were born in total, and seven trees planted, known as the "Seven Sisters". Eventually the longed for son was born, but apparently cursed by a wizard who hated the squire. The lad was sent away to be educated abroad, making the father feel pleased that he had evaded the curse. However, when the lad returned many years later to the Hall, a vicious storm was raging, and the travelling became difficult. He carefully made his way home without hindrance until he reached the seven chestnut trees. Here his carriage was suddenly struck by lightning and totally destroyed, as T.A. Coward says

"each fatal tree was stained with gore."
"The seven sister trees may still be seen,
Though the mortal ones are fled;
And none of that fated house were left,
When the Squire himself was dead."

The wizard's curse seemed to have worked, along with the "just-deserts" he apparently received from the ill-treatment of his daughters.

Fletcher Moss gave an interesting piece of advice in his 1898 work mentioned previously, that was to be very wary when buying old oak furniture, especially grandfather clocks because they would often be made from the wood of old coffins! This was apparently more rife in country areas, where the wonderful dark oak colour of the furniture was achieved in a much shorter time, because the wood had in fact been buried in the ground. One can't help but wonder if these coffins were more easily obtained after the "resurrectionists" had finished their nightly work.

T.A. Coward also had some interesting snippets of information on the subject, relating how old coffins were used on farmsteads as feeding troughs for pigs. But it did not end there, the pigs of Acton's vicarage were actually found to be feeding from the church's long-lost Norman font! This was hastily cleaned up and returned to the church upon discovery.

4

Strange Animals

Phantom hounds are often regarded with dread, as images of the "Hound of the Baskervilles" spring to mind. This may be because of their association with death, and of being omens of disaster. However, in some areas they are thought to be protective spirits, guiding people along dangerous moorland and preventing children from becoming lost on dark nights. Accounts describe the hounds as being ghost-like, with no substance, and the ability to appear and disappear at will. This suggests that it would be impossible for the spectre to physically attack a human being. They were seen mainly around churchyards, crossroads, old lanes and areas of water – all very lonely places, and prone to superstition anyway.

The most well-documented sighting of a ghostly dog in Cheshire was in 1906. A fishmonger from Hyde was returning home from Broadbottom along a lane in Godley Green, when he became aware of something by his side. To his horror, about a yard in front of the roadside hedge, was a huge tan-coloured dog, seemingly the size of a cow! He walked faster and then ran to try to escape the strange hound, but it kept exactly the same pace, never leaving his side. Feeling frightened because he did not understand what this weird animal was, the man lashed out with his fist to hit it. His hand went straight through it and brushed the hedge on the other side! The apparition made no attempt to attack the man, or make any threatening gesture, despite the fishmonger's violent reaction to it. Eventually it walked ahead of him, and then moved backwards like a car reversing, at which point the man fled and was not followed. He described it as "... the most hideous thing I ever saw.

Its feet went pit-a-pat, with a horrible clanking noise, sounding like chains."

Apparently, this was not an isolated incident, as several years beforehand a little girl had been followed in the same manner, and told her mother she had wanted to throw stones at it to make it go away. Her mother warned her against this as it was a phantom hound which might get angry, and tear the little girl to pieces!

It sounds more like the dog was acting as a kind of guide, accompanying the travellers, and maybe protecting them from a very real physical danger they had no knowledge of.

This same dog seemed to frequent an area around a particular house in the locality, as one lady in the 1890s also saw it near a frozen pond, and thought it was an escaped lion. It followed her, but disappeared before she reached her house. She described it as having eyes "as large as saucers" and that the feet went "pit-a-pat" just as the fishmonger had experienced.

Other less well-known cases were a black dog which "galloped at dusk" down the road to Barthomley Rectory, one which haunted the gates of Spurstow Hall, and a white dog near a Bunbury school which was said to be dragging chains.

Phantom hounds are not the only form of large, ghostly animal in Cheshire. There are also many accounts of large cats which cannot be explained.

Handforth was witness to such a strange encounter that it was widely reported in the press at the time. In August 1980 a "cat-like animal" was sighted in the area by a farmer, who at first thought it was a young stag, but when he moved closer he saw it had the form of a cat, and was much larger than any he had ever seen before. He described it as being " the size of an Alsatian with pointed ears, a cat-like body and tail."

Right: a phantom hound in a churchyard setting.

Bunbury School, where a phantom hound was sighted.

The main difference between the ghostly dogs and the large cats or "alien black cats" as they have been nicknamed, is that the dogs were apparitions and the cats were *real*. The majority of sightings came in the 1970s and 1980s, and several were actually killed between 1983-5 in Scotland. It has been suggested that this is indeed a new form of animal, which walks with its claws out, unlike the domestic cat, and is dog-sized with adults measuring around forty-three inches from nose to tail. They are mainly jet-black in colour, with long legs and tail, a slender body, and large fangs.

On 23rd October 1976 in Upton near Chester, it was reported that a lioness had been seen, and then vanished again. The first thought was that one had escaped from Chester Zoo, but after a thorough check it was revealed that none were missing.

The theory explaining the existence of this strange animal, as revealed in Janet and Colin Board's "Modern Mysteries of Britain", begins with the surge of interest in the 1950s and 1960s of large cat, for example pumas, as household pets. By the 1970s the law had been changed to protect such animals from ill-treatment, and many were abandoned. People had also become fed up with the responsibility attached to such large pets (as they still do today with ordinary cats and dogs), and just let them loose to be rid of them. It then becomes a possibility that the strange large cats are the result of a cross-breeding between, for example, a puma, and a wild cat. So is there really a new, giant and fanged breed of cat roaming around Cheshire?

5

Plague in Old Cheshire

There were many times of plague in old England, with the lack of medicine and crude attempts at hygiene doing nothing to curb the transmission of many contagious diseases. In most cases any fatal and fast acting sickness was termed "plague", with little or no description of symptoms. One rather rare, but extremely fast-acting disease was termed "sweating sickness", and attacked the population of Chester in 1507, wiping out ninety-one lives in just three days. Another outbreak occurred in 1551, and it was said that this sickness could develop and kill in just two to three hours. William Axon in his article in "Bygone Cheshire" explained that "some died in the opening of their windows, and others when playing with their children at the street doors." The only clue to any sufferer was the frequent shivering and profuse sweating caused by the disease, but after a couple of hours of this, death occurred swiftly, leaving little chance of any treatment or cure.

The "Black Death" around 1350 was estimated to have claimed twenty five million lives throughout Europe, with Cheshire being no exception to this, although details are scarce. One hint to the devastating effects can be found from Bucklow, where two hundred and fifteen acres of land was evacuated and left desolate, because former tenants in the area had succumbed to the fatal "Black Death". It was not only the crowded cities which suffered, because no produce would be accepted from plague-stricken areas, creating widespread famine and unhygienic "no-go" areas.

Chester seems to have been the worst affected though, with no less than *ten* outbreaks of various plagues between 1507 and 1654. In 1517, the situation was so bad that trade had to abandoned with non-residents, and the grass on the streets grew to foot in length from the lack of traffic upon it.

The Chester residents escaped much more lightly in 1558, when at the hint of another outbreak, many quickly fled the town and managed to escape the deaths. However, in 1574 the town was again ravaged by plague, with the mayor Sir John Savage bringing in swift new regulations to prevent the spread of disease. These began with the stricken houses having to bear the words "Lord have mercy upon us" as a warning to any would-be visitors to the properties. No-one from these houses was allowed to leave the building without prior permission from the Alderman of their ward, and even then they had to carry a token symbolising their danger to the rest of the town. Even with permission, and their token, they still could not leave the house in the hours of darkness, and anyone doing so would be promptly arrested (this must have been very difficult though, bearing in mind their status as an "untouchable"). Extra regulations were introduced to try and improve the sanitation of the streets, with a ban on any dumping of manure or other waste in the city streets, restrictions on the swine-keepers, and a ban on any dogs wandering the streets. Dogs would be shot dead if found outside anyone's house. Any traders wishing to sell their stock in the city, had to leave their goods outside the walls until they had been fully "aired". To add to the distress of the householders with plague victims inside, wooden walls were constructed around some buildings to provide further isolation. This appeared to have been done because many of those stricken were ignoring the earlier regulations.

Chester fell victim to fever again twenty-nine years later in 1603, when the Glover household on St John's Lane produced the initial alarming casualties. From the seven deaths in this house, the figure soon multiplied until up to sixty people a week succumbed to the deadly plague. Again, similar precautions were introduced by the mayor, with the Michaelmas Fair of that year being abandoned entirely. Presumably as a consequence of the last devastation by plague, the mayor also proposed a new plan to isolate the infected, and protect those left in the "danger zone".

Cabins were constructed near the river, for the sole purpose of housing those stricken by the deadly disease. Anyone found with symptoms of plague were hastily conveyed to the makeshift huts, in an attempt to stop the contamination of the whole town. This does not seem to have been any more successful than the previous methods of isolation, because from October 1603 to March 1604 a total of eight hundred and twelve people died in Chester alone.

After two more minor visitations in 1608 and 1610, Chester fell victim to pestilence again in 1647, which ravaged the City more violently than any other time in its history. In just ten months there were two thousand and ninety nine deaths.

Although suffering the majority of plague visitations, Chester was by no means the only Cheshire town devastated by disease. Northwich in 1576 saw the household of Philip Antrobus infected, with most of the occupants dying in a matter of days. This seemed to have been contained though, and after the last death, the linen used on the sick was thrown into a nearby river, even though it was worth a considerable amount of money. This so upset the remaining relatives, that a claim for compensation was later lodged with the local authorities.

Nantwich suffered a more severe outbreak in 1604, the pestilence having been transferred from Chester. In six months the village saw four hundred and thirty members of its population die from plague. The following year saw Stockport become infected, with eight hundred and twelve deaths between 9th October and 20th March 1606. The town's museum still contains a stone bowl which was used on the Market Place to prevent stall-holders becoming victims themselves. When a stranger paid for goods purchased, the money had to be placed in this bowl which was filled with vinegar, therefore killing any germs which may have been unwittingly passed on. These bowls were apparently used throughout Cheshire in such times of fear.

Right: Plague victims

When Malpas received its visitation of plague in 1625, one of the residents performed an admirable act of self sacrifice, to ease the problems of his family left behind. Ralph Dawson apparently returned from London at the end of July, bringing with him the curse of plague and death. By the end of August, both he, his father, mother, and sister had died from the disease, and his uncle became ill with it himself. Being a rather large and heavy man, he became worried that the remaining members of the household (his nephew and a young servant girl) would not be able to carry him to his grave to bury him, without a great deal of struggling and strain to themselves. So thinking, and "perceyveing he must dye at any time", he got up from his bed, went to some waste ground near his house, and began to dig his own grave. He asked his nephew, John Dawson to lay some straw along the bottom of the grave, where he promptly lay down and waited to die. This plague raged in Malpas for another two months, with the remaining members of the Dawson household already sick and soon to pass away.

Congleton had its dose of suffering in December 1641, when plague arrived via a box of clothes from London (other sources say Eyam). During the next two years, cabins similar to those in Chester were erected to try and contain the disease, but again with seemingly little effect. Another self-sacrificing individual made her appearance here though, by the name of "Little Bess" or "Lancashire Bess". Her real name was Elizabeth Smith, and she was known as a sort of Florence Nightingale to the plague-stricken, who were so used to being treated as "unclean" by those afraid of their own well-being. "Little Bess" worked in many plague-stricken areas, bringing comfort to the dying in their hours of need, and being paid small sums by the local authorities to cover her requests for linen and medication.

T.A. Coward in "Picturesque Cheshire" related a tale from a Congleton man which occurred during the town's infestation with plague. Bearing in mind the authorities' reluctance to have anything to do with houses hit by plague, he told them that when he succumbed, he would tie one end of a rope around his leg and trail the other out of the door, so that no one would have to enter such a deadly house. This idea was gratefully received, and when no more sound was heard from the house, and the occupant was thought to have died, the locals found the rope trailing out of the door, and began to pull on it to avoid entering the house. They pulled and pulled until the house itself seemed to move with force and become unstable. Reluctantly they entered, and found that far from being considerate, the old man had played a final joke on them, because the rope was in fact tied to one of the beams of the house!

Along with many other towns, Congleton took precautions against the spread of plague, with an Order being passed with the effect that "watch and ward was taken at every common passage out of the towne and at cross lanes neare adjoyning to keep in ye Townsmen" and the market which was held every Monday, had to be transferred to another location, three quarters of a mile from the town.

The last recorded case from these times of pestilence in old Cheshire comes from Wilmslow, a town previously unmentioned with regard to plague, but obviously not untouched by it, as the fear of contagion is reflected in this account. According to the parish registers, a lady named E. Stanow returned to her Wilmslow home already showing great signs of illness. She suffered this ailment out in her own home and died from its effects on the following day, July 17th 1665. The townsfolk were so suspicious of the cause of her death that they buried her in unconsecrated ground by her home, trying to avoid any new infestation of plague in their town. The grave remained as a reminder to future generations of the devastation plague could cause, if not isolated in time, and stood alone in open ground near Lindow Common.

After the Great Fire of London which effectively wiped out the deadly plague in the capital, there were no more recorded cases in old Cheshire, suggesting that the populace had eventually learned from their mistakes, and paid more attention to the hygiene of the streets and houses, wiping out the deadly plagues forever.

In more recent years, the Industrial Revolution provoked more widespread disease, although by 1865, it was no longer called "plague". The terrible living conditions, increased population, and general state of poor health in the new industrial areas gave rise to the spread of Cholera and other fatal illnesses. Winsford was one such example, suffering an outbreak in 1865 which continued claiming lives into the following year. The influx of foreign workers for the salt mines was blamed, because hundreds of families were living in such poor conditions that there were no facilities to deal with an epidemic, and no money around for them to have lived as hygienically as they would have liked.

By the turn of this century "plague" as our ancestors had known it had been effectively been wiped out, so you can imagine the panic of Macclesfield's population in 1919 when an outbreak of Smallpox threatened the lives of everyone in the district. News spread quickly in the town throughout August, when the outbreak was first identified, but quick thinking and fast actions soon eradicated the problem, clearing up all traces of the disease, and preventing any transference to other areas.

Bearing in mind the details of the past chapter, we of the Twentieth Century pride ourselves in our understanding of contagious diseases, standing back with a moralising attitude to criticise our ancestors for their lack of hygiene which increased the spread of contagious diseases. One last detail which may put things in proportion, is the recent spread of AIDS which has instilled panic and prejudice rather than understanding and sympathy. It is exactly these attitudes that allowed our ancestors to suffer the ravages of plague, and it seems, unfortunately, that the lesson still has not been learned; meaning that we ourselves could tomorrow be victim to a "plague", not because we don't know what caused it, but because we insist on segregating, and blaming the persons it attacks as if they *invited* their own death.

6

Witchcraft and Possession

The practice of witchcraft was rife in Cheshire, as with other parts of the country, but the meaning of the word has changed over the centuries to present a different image of what was, fundamentally derived from the original religion in Britain. With the advent of the Christian Church (many thousands of years after witchcraft, or Paganism as it was then generally known), witchcraft had to be outlawed. So consequently what was just a celebration of, and working in harmony with, nature became evil, demonic, and classified as "devil worship" (the fact that the Pagans never even acknowledged the existence of a "devil" seemed to be unimportant). However, the Christian church did successfully alter the original Pagan festivals into their own celebrations, with the exception of Samhain or Hallowe'en, which they are still trying to ban even today! As a consequence Yule became Christmas, the Spring Equinox or Eostra became Easter, and Imbolc became Candlemass.

Even though people are becoming more open minded in the Twentieth Century, the image of Pagans or witches as evil, still exists. This is probably due to the Satanists, who also only came into existence with the formation of the Christian church. Satanists reverse everything the Christian church teaches, e.g.. black masses and inverted crosses. Pagans follow their Old Religion, but have unfortunately been the victims of a general lack of understanding, with many people believing that a Pagan is actually a Satanist!

During the fury of the witch burnings, the same mistake was often made, with a few genuine practitioners of black magic being rightfully accused, but unfortunately the majority of executions

93

took place on innocent people, who perhaps worked with herbs as medicines, used white magic for healing, or even had a wart in an unsightly place or were left handed! This difference must be established before I relate the following accounts, so that the narrow minded fears from the past do not cloud our judgement in the present.

Crossroads were widely regarded as meeting places for witches, mainly because of their already well-established reputation of being lonely, spooky places. Gibbets often hung there with rotting corpses inside, and so anyone who frequented such places was regarded with suspicion. The association with Diana, or Hecate of the three ways, the goddess reputed to guard crossroads and also a divinity worshipped by witches (most notably in Shakespeare's "Macbeth"), also made crossroads a prime site for sabbats.

More specifically, in Cheshire Alderley Edge has long been associated with witches and sorcerers, the most famous being King Arthur's Merlin. The Edge has supposedly been a site for ritual worship since the Bronze Age, following through right up until today, its reputation being equated with that of Pendle Hill in Lancashire. Mrs. Joan Rogers, a white witch from Denton, Manchester, says that Alderley today seems to have some sort of time-slip phenomenon, with ancient images superimposing themselves on the modern day. Apart from that, the Edge does seem to have an "atmosphere" conducive to psychic phenomenon, with reports of ghosts and mysterious winds, noises and "presences". It has been suggested that Ley Lines cross in this area, prompting such psychic manifestations, but no definite proof has ever been presented, despite many studies of the subject.

Witchcraft: fiction and fact

M.G.Mills ©1994

An account exists of a woman accused of witchcraft in Holmes Chapel in 1592. Mrs. Jackson was suspected of such practices because she was known to heal cattle, and cure children of various illnesses. Despite her helpful role in society, the fact that her methods were not understood by everyone else led her to be accused of witchcraft. She denied this, but was brought before the court because she did not stop her healing activities. This time, she admitted it,(the use of torture for confessions was widespread, but not recorded as diligently as the trials were. Consequently, such sudden confessions were far from rare). The court ruled that she must make the same confession to the congregation at her local church on 18th October that same year.

A happier account from Church Coppenhall in the Eighteenth Century, shows that not all the populace were fearful of beneficial healing powers, and actually took advantage of Bridget Bostock's skills. Although anxious not to be called a witch in such dangerous times, Bridget was called the "Cheshire Inspiration Doctress". She had supporters nationwide, with letters about her appearing in the "Gentleman's Magazine" in 1748. She could remove warts using prayer and saliva, and was known for general healing as well as her skill in exorcising devils from victims of possession. She never charged for her activities, but welcomed donations, just as White Witches do today, as some believe that charging a fee would diminish the power of the spell or cure. Regular patients came from Middlewich and Nantwich, and even further afield, and she is said to have had up to 160 patients a week seeking her expertise. It was probably her talent for exorcism, and use of prayer that saved her from being regarded as an "evil witch".

Congleton also possessed a natural healer, whose talents were widely recognised, and in great demand when she was just 13 years old. She was especially noted for her skill of easing the pain in bad burns and scalds.

Charles Bradbury was also known as a healer, and had hundreds of sick people seek his expertise, mainly in charming away jaundice.

Another local witch was said to have cured one of the Baileys of

Etchells, who was suffering from an infection in his hip. This was done by the use of various charms, and by passing him through a split rowan tree.

Robert Nixon, the famous Cheshire prophet was said to have been born at Bridge End house in Over, although no parish records sustantiate this. Described by T.A. Coward as "a short, squab fellow, had a great head and goggle eyes; that he used to drivel as he spoke, which was very rarely, and was extremely sulky and half-witted." He was also said to have hated children, whom he regularly beat if they came near him, and had to be beaten himself before he would do any work.

His skills as a prophet became apparent one day when he was working on his brother's plough, and beating the oxen too hard. His fellow worker threatened to tell the boss about this ill-treatment, but Nixon merely said that it wouldn't do any good because "the beast would not be his brother's in three days". Sure enough, on the third day the cattle were taken by the Lord of the manor, leaving his brother without sufficient beasts to plough his land. Another prophecy of his which has been remembered relates to the household of Vale Royal. The Cholmondeley family badly needed an heir to continue their family name, and Nixon declared that this would only happen when an eagle visited the house. Thousands of people saw an eagle near the house around the birth of the next child, which did indeed turn out to be a little boy. The eagle remained near the house for three days, then stayed around the village for three days before disappearing. Mrs. Cholmondeley's sister, Mrs. Chute claimed it was the "biggest bird she had ever seen". This lady and others tried to frighten it off for some reason, but "it refused to budge 'till the little babe arrived". From this legend follows the tradition that an eagle should be kept on the grounds at all times, so that the resident family would never want for an heir.

Nixon predicted many other minor events in the district, but Royal recognition soon came when he successfully predicted the outcome of the battle of Bosworth. The King offered him a place in Court, but he became very upset at this, insisting that he would starve to death there. Such a request though was virtually impossible to refuse, and upon arrival at Hampton Court, the King asked him to find a lost ring. This was intended to trick Nixon as the ring had actually been hidden for this express purpose. However, His Majesty was very impressed with the prophet's answer – "He who hideth, can find". Having passed this test, Nixon related his fears of being starved, and the King permitted him to live in the kitchens, and to eat as much as he wanted, whenever he wanted.

Nixon had a "great appetite", and took full advantage of his new situation, to the disgust of the kitchen staff, who hated his constant picking at the meat. This continued for such a long time, that the irritation grew too much for the staff, who one day locked him in a cupboard for a bit of peace and quiet. Somehow, he was forgotten, and true to his prophecy, he starved to death, tortured by the constant smells of food emanating from the kitchen. Again, as with his birthplace and date, there are no records to place this death, so it is a matter for great debate as to the exact period Nixon lived in. Documentation on his prophecies is too much to be ignored, so it seems that this man really did exist at some time in Cheshire's history.

Black Magic

Moving onto the more obvious sources of fear and association with black magic, the story of an elaborate curse comes from Bunbury. Image House on Whitchurch Road boasts a Seventeenth Century cottage, which has carved stone figures wearing cocked hats on the walls and in the garden. The story behind these, is that over one hundred years ago a poacher (who had also shot a keeper by mistake) was sentenced to transportation and served his term, pledging to seek vengeance on those officials that convicted him. He returned to England after his sentence expired, and began to dabble in black magic, in his home in Bunbury. The rest of his life was spent carving the stone images of the Sheriff and officials he wished to avenge. As he completed these, he cursed them and left them in his garden as a sign to the men that he would never forget them, and wished them many misfortunes. It is doubtful that the curse physically worked, but psychologically, it must have been very successful, as the cursed men would feel uncomfortable, and probably wonder if any mishaps in their daily life were as a result of the poacher's hatred. Other stone figures were added later by a new resident, including the images of two jackdaws, a fox and a hideous face.

More comical, is another tale from Alderley Edge. The Manchester Evening News received an account from a girl who had attended a Hallowe'en party there, and claimed to have seen a man change into a goat! She said that his face suddenly changed and became very hairy, his eyes turned to a yellow colour, and he grew horns on his head! No other witnesses reported the remarkable transformation, but she maintained that she had been extremely frightened. It is not clear whether the party was a fancy dress, or if the girl had consumed much alcohol.

Possession

In 1602, Thomas Harrison of Northwich provoked much controversy and interest. He was reputed to be possessed by a demon. Many local officials witnessed him shaking his head violently for long periods of time, exhibiting great physical strength and then losing consciousness completely. More significantly though, he was heard speaking in different voices, and languages of which he previously had no knowledge.

The whole community was invited to pray for his recovery, and seven preachers were assigned to help him personally. They used a variety of methods for exorcism, including private prayer and fasting. Surprisingly in the Seventeenth Century, the bishop was not keen on running along with public opinion, and had the case investigated thoroughly before allowing any attempts at exorcism by his priests. The symptoms were indeed spectacular, and many who witnessed them did not believe that a human could utter such noises without supernatural aid. The affliction was blamed on "local witches", who had supposedly cursed Thomas or invited the devil to possess his body, although no one was named or brought to trial. Doctors were also consulted, and attributed his condition to "an excess of some Melancholia".

The verdict remained open, as the details of how and when (or if) Thomas recovered were not recorded.

Another case of suspected possession occurred in Chester. Eighteen year old Anne Milner was bringing the cattle in from a field on her father's farm, when she found herself being surrounded by a white form, which she took to be an evil spirit. This experience so upset Anne that she became ill the next day, and was confined to bed. She became the victim of death-like trances, and supposedly exhibited symptoms akin to those of demonic possession. The "illness" continued for a month when it was suddenly cured by a priest, Master Lane, who forced her to say the Lord's Prayer and blessed her. Further investigation into the case reached the conclusion that it had been caused by an "elemental guardian", a sort of powerful apparition which is invoked to guard a sacred place from unwanted intrusion.

Charms

With all these strange and frightening things happening to the superstitious people of old Cheshire, it is no wonder that many methods were employed to protect against witchcraft and possession. Bridget Bostock, as I have said, was actively involved in healing persons victim to possession, as was another white witch, or wizard called John from Hale Barns, known as John o' th' Hill. He was called in to quieten a witch in Castle Mill, which he did by making an image of her, putting nine pins in it and a nail from a horse shoe. Together with a toad, this was bundled into a bottle, and buried by the wizard, who also said various prayers or charms to ward off the witch's powers. It seemed to have worked, as no more complaints were received.

A more interesting charm against witches, and one which it was possible to keep in your house was an old parson's wig. These were said to be holy, and have the power to turn away any witch who tried to enter the house in the guise of an animal or other creature. Standon Hall used to have such a wig hung over the fireplace to prevent any witch gaining access this way.

It was also common practice to believe that something had been bewitched if it didn't go to plan. Even butter could be bewitched if it did not churn properly. In these cases any local person who seemed a little odd, or had shown a dislike to the victim would be accused of having cast the spell.

7

Punishments and Torture

Punishments and torture in old Cheshire were among the most brutal in the country. The Stockport brank, for example, is widely known for its vicious construction, designed to inflict as much pain as possible upon the wearer and provide engrossing entertainment for the hundreds of onlookers. It is interesting to note that some of the keenest observers (often at the front of the crowd at hangings) were children.

One of the oldest records of a ducking stool in Cheshire is from the Domesday Book (1084), which reports the existence of at least one of them in Chester city centre. Women would be tied to a chair and lowered into the water as punishment for a variety of crimes regarded as insignificant nowadays. In 1184, Chester was known to use the ducking stool for men and women who cheated customers by selling short measures, although this could be avoided by payment of a heavy fine.

Nantwich's ducking stool was erected at Cartlake Lane in 1592, but only after fire had destroyed the old one nearly ten years prior to this. The old stool was located by the town's cess pool, so the new one was probably seen as a big improvement!

Knutsford had two ducking stools, one in the Higher, and one in the Lower parts of town, and in 1605, Margaret Danatt was said to be "doing penance", after having been declared "a common scold and disturber of her neighbours", although what her punishment was exactly, is not mentioned. It was not unknown for women to be ducked on the stool and have to wear a brank at the same time.

Most widely used for the punishment of women was the brank,

or scold's bridle. This consisted of a cage-like helmet fastened to the head, with a mouth-piece to curb the tongue. There were many variations, the most brutal being in Stockport, where the two inch mouth-piece ended in a ball with three iron spikes above, three below, and two at the back, which was guarantied to painfully rip into the tongue, as the woman was led around the Market Place. To make it worse still, it was the only brank to have the pulling chain at the front rather than the back of the head, ensuring maximum movement of the spikes inside the mouth. Apart from the obvious pain inflicted by this instrument, the tongue would swell up afterwards leaving the woman in agony for many days. It was also known for women to contract blood-poisoning from their wounds, with the brank probably never being cleaned from victim to victim. On market days it would be hung on display as a warning to stall-holders not to cheat their customers, and for women not express any grievances against officials, neighbours or their husbands, or to use any bad language.

The Stockport Brank

The earliest known use of a brank was in Macclesfield in 1623, where they specifically singled out prostitutes and women of "lighte behaviour and loose morals." This was a much more humane bridle with a plain tongue-piece, and just one band passing over the head to keep it in place. There was also the opportunity of changing the dimension to fit any head, therefore making it more comfortable.

The Macclesfield Brank

Congleton used their brank in a rather unique way. If a wife was scolding her husband or using bad language, he could call for the town gaoler who would arrive with the scold's bridle, put it on the outspoken wife, and hook the whole thing up to the fireplace, where she would have to remain until her husband saw fit. Each fireplace in the area apparently had a hook expressly for this purpose, and if a husband became angry with his wife, he would point at the hook, and the threat alone would be enough to silence most women!

Opposite: a victim of the Stockport brank.

M.G.Mills © 1994

The Congleton Brank

However, the last recorded use of the brank in Congleton was more traditional, with the lady being paraded around the streets in 1824. Ann Runcorn was brought before the courts because of her outspoken reaction to the churchwardens, who were doing their rounds of the public houses on a Sunday, to make sure they were all closed during services. She was reported to have met them near the "Cockshoot", and told them that they were all villains and rogues (or words to that effect!) and said "it would look better of them if they would look after their own houses rather than go looking after other folks, which were far better than their own", within earshot of a witness who gave evidence against her. She was sentenced to "there and then have the town's bridle for scolding women put upon her, and that she be led by the magistrates' clerk's clerk through every street in the town, as an example to all scolding women." A man called Prosper Haslem did indeed carry out the sentence, and she was released afterwards outside the Town Hall in front of the Mayor, and most of the town's occupants. This does not seem to have curbed her tongue though, because as soon as it was removed, she declared "I'll be damned if I won't do it again the next time I see you going round, for you deserve more than I have given you, and I'll do it again!"

Mercifully, the Congleton brank was of similar design to the Macclesfield one, the punishment being one of embarrassment and humiliation, rather than pain.

Altrincham's last use of the brank was in 1820 on an old woman who had frequently been threatened with it, but continued using bad language, insulting her neighbours and causing minor disturbances. She was sentenced to walk through the town wearing the bridle, but refused to move an inch so was carted round in a wheelbarrow instead! This seems to have worked, because it is said that the town experienced no more trouble from the meddling woman, and that she "ever afterwards kept a civil and respectful tongue in her head."

Warrington's last recorded use of the instrument was also on a notorious scold and resident of the workhouse, Cicily Pewsill in the early 1800s. She was forced to wear the brank for over half an hour along the city street, causing her the utmost embarrassment, and hopefully quietening her tongue.

Although there are no direct accounts from Chester, the city made branks for many other towns, and a total of *four* for their own use!

Stocks and Pillories

The ducking stool and brank were not the only punishments for criticising your neighbours, or having a sharp tongue. Many women were also put in the stocks or pillory for the same crimes, but these very public punishments were used for a much wider variety of offences, and on men as well as women. Crimes for the stocks and pillory ranged from drunkenness to homelessness, and further back in time even breaking the Sabbath was regarded as an offence punishable by this public humiliation.

Tramps especially were targeted, mainly so that they would

leave the village and not come back. If they did return, a worse sentence would be passed upon them. The stocks would usually be in the centre of the town or village to attract as much attention as possible, and act as a warning to others. Grappenhall's stocks stood just outside the church, and Stockport's were once located on the Market Place but have been preserved, and now stand in the courtyard at Bramall Hall. Warrington's stocks were even more orientated to the public's enjoyment of punishments, being fixed to a set of wheels which could then be used to parade the offender around the busiest parts of the town. In addition these mobile stocks could fit four people in at once, compared to most which only accommodated one prisoner.

The year of 1822 saw two women in the Stockport stocks, one for being drunk and the other for spreading scandal about her neighbours. They seem to have got off lightly, as their three hour stretch in the stocks was much preferable to the gruesome brank of that area which was also used for these offences. In 1849, Thomas Leah actually spent all night in the stocks at Bramhall.

Further back in history of course, the punishments were more severe, and in 1495 a tramp would have to spend three days and nights in the stocks, and six if he were discovered again in the same village.

However, when John, a bandsman in Middleton was confined to the stocks, his stay was not so much a punishment as a continuance of his celebrations, as the rest of the band gathered round and began playing music, which many other locals sang to and began dancing in time with.

On many occasions the public did take pity on individuals in the stocks, but in the Fifteenth Century, if they were to feed the prisoner or give them a drink at all, then they could face a fine by the local authorities. Just as people took sympathy on those imprisoned publicly, there were also many others who used the felon as a target for verbal and physical abuse, making the sentence of time in the stocks a physically painful and mentally damaging punishment. In many cases the misdemeanour was not

The stocks at Lymm

repeated – a threat of a second spell in the stocks was not be dismissed lightly!

As if these weren't enough, Cheshire towns and villages also used public whipping posts for punishment of virtually the same crimes. Middlewich townsfolk witnessed public whippings of tramps on market days in the Bull Ring, and Stockport folk had the same gruesome spectacle right next to the Market Place.

In most cases, these methods were used merely to embarrass and humiliate the offender, but sometimes they increased greatly in barbarity, maybe for more serious or persistent offenders, or perhaps depending upon the mentality of the officials and residents of the town, at particular periods in history.

Such diversity in sentencing came about because the individual corporations in the towns were allowed to pass their own sentences on any crimes that were not recognised by the law of the land. This mainly related to crimes in moral behaviour, than those of say, stealing.

One crime which would be punished solely by the Lord of the Manor though, was that of poaching. If a felon was found guilty of this, or left the village in fear of prosecution, the forester and Lord shared out his belongings between them. This included everything in his possession from his livestock to the cooking utensils in the house.

Prisons and penal conditions

The findings of James Neild in the Eighteenth Century tells us a lot about the state of the prisons of the time, and what went on there. When Neild investigated Chester Gaol, he found a prisoner with irons on his legs, waist and neck, which connected to a long spike which ran down his back. These extra precautions were added because the man had tried to escape. The gaoler said they had been in place for two months, but the prisoner insisted it had been three months.

Many prisoners refused to plead because if they were found

guilty then their possessions would be taken away. Most wished to save their meagre belongings for their family to inherit, and so refused to talk. This prompted many hideous and painful devices to be used to try and break their silence. Adam of the Woodhouses was one such man who didn't want his possessions taken away, and had burnt his house and hidden his belongings. He was allowed three morsels of bread on one day, and "three sips from the nearest puddle the next". This seemed to have no effect on the stubborn man, so "to accelerate the man's decision" the King (Edward II), originated the idea of putting heavy weights upon his chest. Adam was crushed to death during the process. During the reign of Edward III, things seemed no better, as a report revealed that one gaoler had put too many irons on a prisoner, put him in the stocks, and abused him to such an extent that the man died. This deputy constable was "hauled over the coals" as a punishment for what was in effect, murder.

In 1806 a Macclesfield man was found to have been imprisoned for six months for a debt of five shillings and three pence, but the same sentence was given to a man who owed just nine pence! Their stay would not have been a pleasant one as the cell was in a very bad condition, and was six inches deep in mud.

Another prison reformer who made such investigations was John Howard. He visited Chester Gaol in 1788, and found instruments of torture such as thumbscrews and a "necklet", an iron band for the throat with sharp metal spikes on the inside! He also reported on a Nantwich workhouse in the same year, and found that the inmates were allowed five shillings a month for tobacco and snuff, but if anyone was found to possess any tea (even when bought with their own money), they were to be punished by a spell in the dungeon!

Excommunication

To many, these physical punishments and deprivations were nothing when compared the threat of excommunication. One would think that such a drastic action would only occur if someone had committed a crime that was too terrible for even God to forgive them for, but this wasn't the case. A document dated 31st October 1442, from the Archdeacon of Chester, said that anyone who had chopped down trees from the woods of Thomas de Legh of Northwood and Knutsford, or had been fishing in his ponds, stolen from his house "and done him other injuries" was to be warned three times, and if they did not replace these items within fifteen days (rather difficult if fish had been eaten, or wood used on a fire), then they were to publicly excommunicated. This is just a further example of the rather severe punishments used for, what now seem to us, minor misdemeanours.

8

Murders and Gibbets

The November 1963 issue of "Cheshire Life" magazine carried a detailed account of a murder committed almost one hundred years beforehand. It concerned a young woman named Alice Bailey, who lived in Stockport with her elderly mother, Mary, who needed much attention; and a man named George Holt whose name Alice adopted, and lived with as if married.

Alice became tired of looking after her sick mother and wanted to live in peace with her partner George, but any plots to "eliminate" Mary would be financially unprofitable, as the lady was not insured, and would be unable to pass any medical examinations needed to provide cover anyway. Alice was undeterred by this fact and persuaded a friend, Betty Wood, to stand in for Mary in an interview with an insurance company. Alice told Betty that this was commonplace, and that "anyone would do", so the examination went ahead without a hitch, and insurance cover for twenty-six pounds, payable upon death, was provided.

With the prospect of some extra money, and a life free of her invalid mother, Alice then began to plot Mary's murder. The first idea was simply to withhold the medicines from her mother, and hope that her condition would deteriorate, and soon bring on death. Mary was a strong woman though, despite her illness, and this appeared to have no effect, or would take such a long time that Alice had to think of a quicker way. George suggested that they light some charcoal underneath Mary's bed, in the hope that the fumes would kill her, but this had an obvious drawback in the fact that it could burn the whole house down! This plan was soon abandoned.

Becoming more frustrated with the situation, Alice bought a large amount of arsenic, claiming that it was to kill rats. On 26th February 1863, Alice put some of the deadly poison into her mother's drink. The effect was immediate, and the old woman soon lay dead at her daughter's hand. She was buried shortly afterwards, with no one suspecting foul play.

The plan seemed to have worked to perfection until several weeks later when Alice's sister Ann discovered the arsenic, still in the bottom of her late mother's cup. The insurance company was informed of this possible fraud, and had Mary's body exhumed and examined for the true cause of death. The results revealed that there were 160 grains of arsenic in the old woman's body – 80 times the dose needed to kill someone!

When Alice was arrested, she was carrying George's child, so the trial had to be postponed. George had conveniently disappeared, and her only visitor during her six months stay in gaol was by his uncle, who adopted the new baby.

Throughout the whole affair, Alice blamed George for the murder, and claimed that she was totally innocent. George was never called upon to give evidence as the judge seemed satisfied of her guilt. She was sentenced to death, and taken to Chester City Gaol, where on the 28th December 1863, she was hanged. However, her death was far from quick, because when the hangman (a man named Calcraft) dropped the trapdoor, it only came part way open and had to be pulled the rest of the way. This meant that Alice did not fall fast enough for her neck to break, but hung for two or three minutes, slowly being strangled to death by her own weight. This greatly excited the crowd of over a thousand people, who had gathered to see the last woman ever to be hanged in public.

The year of 1790 saw a brutal murder in a run-down district of Stockport. Hillgate was once regarded as the red-light area of the town because of the many slums and terrible living conditions, which forced some of the people to seek refuge and enjoyment in drink, and women to try and earn extra money by prostitution. John Dean lived in Watson Square in the centre of the poverty-stricken area, with his wife and five children struggling to survive in one room of a ramshackle tenement building. Like many of the residents, Dean frequented the dubious public houses and enjoyed the company of the "ladies of the night". One particular lady "of easy virtue" as Fletcher Moss (a local historian and writer of the last century) described her, was Sal Fogg from Cheadle, who was rumoured to have requested Dean on several occasions to either leave or "do away with" his wife. Presumably they had a relationship, and Sal wanted it to become more permanent.

One particular night, he returned home very late, and very drunk. His wife (who was three months pregnant), was angrily awaiting his return, upset with Dean's lack of concern for her and the children, and his habit of spending what little money they had on alcohol and other women. An argument broke out, and quickly turned violent, with Dean grabbing a hand brush and beating his wife around the head with it. The children, woken by their mother's screams, looked on in horror as Dean continued beating until she fell lifeless to the floor.

Neighbours had also been awoken by the screams and came running to help, but they were too late. When he realised what he had done, Dean burst out of the house and ran off, now with his own life at stake. His efforts to evade capture were in vain, and he soon found himself imprisoned in the town's dungeon, on Mealhouse Brow near the Market Place. Just days later, he was taken to Chester where he was tried, and found guilty of his wife and unborn child's murder. He was sentenced to be hung and then gibbeted, as an extra warning to others who may have been tempted to commit a similar crime. After being executed in Chester, his body was brought back to Stockport to hang in its iron cage on Black Lake, the area now known as Cherry Tree Lane.

As with all punishments, a large crowd eagerly awaited the gruesome spectacle, and actually followed the cart carrying him for about one and a half miles to its destination! The body had already been encased in the gibbet cage, and would be hung high at a lonely spot (usually crossroads) for many years as the body slowly rotted away. The corpse would be attacked by hungry birds and parasites, until it was picked clean or taken down by the locals.

John Dean's corpse was suspended at Black Lake for many years, forcing the locals to avoid the spot at all costs. The smell alone must have been enough to persuade anyone to find an alternative route home! Fletcher Moss in his "Folklore, Old Customs and Tales" tells of a man who " when a boy, had gone to see the murderer's body on the gibbet and thrown a stone at it. The results of the stone-throwing were rather startling, plainly showing that flies were no respecters of persons".

Eventually, neighbours cut the cage down, burnt the poles, and sold the irons to a blacksmith. This was probably done more for their own peace of mind than out of any sympathy for the murderer.

Another morbid gathering took place in 1731 a few miles from Macclesfield, at a place named Gun Hill, where another murderer was gibbeted in front of a large crowd.

John Naden was found guilty of murdering his employer, a man named Robert Brough, with the aid of Brough's wife, who was rumoured to be Naden's lover. One night, after having consumed much alcohol, Naden stabbed his boss to death and rushed to the house of Mrs. Brough, who immediately ran out to the body and tried to make it look as if a gang of robbers had attacked him. Unfortunately for Naden, she failed to notice the knife he had left behind, which served as evidence that he had committed the crime. This fact, coupled to his lack of an alibi, culminated in his execution by hanging, right outside the door of the widow Brough.

As was the custom with most murderers, he was denied a Christian burial, and further disgraced by having his rotting corpse hung on display in the gibbet irons. This particular cage on Gun Hill remained in place for almost one hundred and fifty years, until it was finally removed in the 1880s, and the wooden stand was used to construct a stile. This stile is said to be haunted by Naden's ghost, who incidentally still hasn't sobered up! The drunken spectre is said to lunge at passers-by in the dark, frightening them away from the stile.

Opposite: the gibbet

Thomas Middleton in his "Legends of Longdendale" recounted a fascinating but tragic tale from the area, which occurred in the late 1700s.

The story goes that a wicked sheriff, also a local landowner, took a lustful fancy to a young woman who worked for him. She rejected his advances adamantly, and provoked his malice to such an extent that one day , as she was working, he insulted her publicly. Her husband was nearby, and took great offence at his taunts, and made to attack the sheriff. He was instantly sacked, along with his wife, leaving them and their child destitute, and close to starvation. Reduced to begging for work and food, the husband desperately tried to feed his wife and child, and one day hunted and shot one of the King's deer in an attempt to relieve their hunger.

Unfortunately, the sheriff heard of this, and instantly arrested the man, demanding that the usual sentence of the time for poaching, be enforced – hanging and gibbeting. The luckless man was duly taken to Gallow's Clough near Mottram, overlooking what is now the A6018 to Stalybridge. Here, he was displayed to an eager crowd as his conviction was read out. At this point his wife could stand no more, and rushed forward pleading with the sheriff to spare his life. The cold-hearted man told the hangman to continue, and threatened the woman with the ducking-stool if she continued to cause a disturbance. Driven half-mad with grief, she broke free of the crowd and ran up to the gallows, where she passionately kissed her husband goodbye. Before she could be stopped, she ran off to the moors, laughing hysterically. The trapdoor of the gallows was immediately released, and her husband hung lifeless from the noose.

By the time darkness fell, his body was already suspended in the gibbet cage, and the young woman returned from the moors to sit by the corpse, singing and talking to it as if he were still alive. Any birds which flew down to pick at the body, were quickly frightened away by her desperate screams. She continued like this until she collapsed with exhaustion close to dawn.

She was disturbed from her sleep by an old woman, who stood by the cage with a knife, and was in the process of removing the dead man's hand. Horrified, the wife explained who she was, and demanded to know what the old woman was doing. She said that she was a practitioner of the black arts, and wanted to construct a hand of glory, and also wanted some fat for other spells. She saw little point in letting it go to waste with the birds picking away, and spoke of the revenge she could achieve against her enemies. Here, the young widow began to show an interest, and told the witch her tale, and of her concern for her sick child who was lying in a bundle underneath the cage. The witch promised to help the woman in her revenge, and the three of them left together, taking the dead man's hand to aid them in their spells.

Several days later, the sheriff's house was in turmoil because his own child had disappeared during the night. A thorough search of the area produced the body of a tiny child, the face so disfigured that it was presumed an animal had attacked it. As a consequence, no definite identification could be made, but it was widely accepted that this was the sheriff's child. The sheriff himself believed that some animal and stolen his child while under an evil spell. His wife was so shocked she fell ill and became an invalid, and the couple never had any more children. The events had such an impact on the sheriff that he became even more callous, and was widely feared by all the townsfolk.

The widow lived in a hut in the woods with her son and the witch, feared by the townspeople who thought that she had also become adept in the black arts. Her son grew into a healthy and handsome young man, but was trained by his mother to become a very skilled thief and criminal. His favourite target was the sheriff's house, and as his raids became more adventurous, a reward was offered for his capture.

Eventually the old witch revealed the whereabouts of the villain, and the enraged sheriff had him arrested and sentenced to death by hanging. The widow and the old witch watched in the crowd as the sheriff gleefully hung the young thief. Then suddenly the woman rushed forward and declared the sheriff to be insane, as he had just killed his own son. She related how her own child had died naturally the same night as her late husband, and of how she used black magic to kidnap the sheriff's son, and reared him as a criminal for this very day. The child buried in the rich family's plot was in fact her own, disguised to avoid suspicion.

The presence of a birthmark on the hanged man's body proved that her story was true, and the sheriff collapsed in horror. The widow laughed loudly, and before she could be arrested, swallowed a lethal dose of poison. The old witch was allowed to pass through the frightened crowd unharmed, pleased with the success of her own, and the widow's vengeance.

Considering how long the corpses had to remain suspended in their lonely spot, several efforts were made to preserve the corpse before it was hung on the gibbet. The most common method was to disembowel the corpse, and then submerge it in boiling pitch which would coat the body and consequently delay decomposition.

Gibbets of Cheshire

Gibbeting was introduced in the early Seventeenth Century, and increased in popularity in 1752 after the "Act for Better Preventing the Horrid Crime of Murder". This Act basically stated that as hanging was the punishment for many crimes, then another, more severe sentence had to be available to deter would-be murderers from committing the crime. The conclusion was that if murderers were denied their dignity after death, and also forbidden a Christian burial, the crime would stand out as much worse than other hanging offences, like stealing. The Eighteenth Century officialdom had no trouble in creating undignified additions to the murderer's sentence, the most dreaded being that of dissection by a doctor for medical research, in a large room full of curious students and sometimes even the general public.

There were many gibbets in old Cheshire, but only a few have been preserved and are in museums for the public to view. One such cage is in Warrington museum, complete apart from the head piece. It was found in 1845 after having been buried at the foot of the gibbet-post in Woolston, where the brutal murder of a postman occurred in 1791. Two years later, Edward Miles was hanged for the robbery and murder, and then unceremoniously returned to the spot two days later in his iron cage, where he remained for many years.

Another gibbet hung on the Chester-Warrington road at Trafford Green, in a place known locally as Gibbet Field. This double gibbet contained the bodies of two local villains, Price and Brown, executed in Boughton in 1796 for highway robbery. The cage was removed in 1820, and it is said that a robin's nest was found inside the remains of Price's skull! A witty little poem contained in T.A. Coward's "Picturesque Cheshire" describes the scene

"Oh! James Price deserves his fate:
Naught but robbing in his pate
Whilst alive, and now he's dead
Has still Robin in his head.
High he swings for robbing the mail,
But his brain of Robin female
Still is quite full; though out of breath,
The passion e'en survives his death."

The practice of gibbeting became virtually non-existent after the turn of the century, with the last Englishman hung in this fashion in 1832 at Leicester, and the custom formally abolished in this country in 1834.

9

The Resurrectionists

During the early 1800s bodysnatching for medical research was rife throughout the country. Cheshire saw its fair share of the crime, with a good market for corpses in the Manchester colleges.

This crime, made famous (or infamous) by the Scottish murderers Burke and Hare, was brought about by a lack of subjects for medical research. The bodies of hung murderers were allocated to the schools, and acted as an extra deterrent to murder in the days when you could be hung for some very minor offences, hence the saying "I may as well be hung for a sheep as a lamb". This extra deterrent was introduced in 1752 by an Act of Parliament for "better preventing the horrid Crime of Murder" which allowed dissection as a substitute for gibbeting (see previous chapter). The Chester surgeon Griffith Rowlands received a body in May 1810, and promptly began his dissection watched by a large public audience! However, although this appeared to be a help to the medical researchers, Charles II was typical of the authorities by allowing only six bodies a year to be given to the medical schools. This obviously necessitated an alternative means of obtaining corpses for study.

Bodysnatching from graves dates back to at least the Seventeenth Century, because William Shakespeare's epitaph from 1616 expresses fear of such an occurrence.

Good friend, for Jesus sake forbeare
To digge the dust enclosed heare.
Bleste be ye man spares these stones,
And curste be he moves my bones.

It began with the surgeons and pupils "obtaining" their own subjects, but as it became more widespread and opposition increased, they couldn't risk doing it themselves, and had to employ some rather shady characters to help.

A point that must be made for you to bear in mind, is that stealing a corpse wasn't actually a crime, as the body was not seen legally as "property". Only if the shroud or coffin were taken as well, had a crime been committed, because they *were* seen as "property". As a consequence, the body-snatchers would leave the shroud and coffin behind, committing no legal crime, but incurring the abhorrence of the neighbourhood.

There were several methods employed by the body-snatchers in their gruesome work. The most common was reminiscent of the scenes from Hammer Horror films. Under cover of darkness the men would usually choose a freshly filled grave, because it made digging easier and quicker. They dug a hole (using wooden shovels to keep the noise down) at the head of the coffin, and then covered the lid with canvas sacking again for silence when they prized the lid off, usually with a crow-bar or hooks. A noose was then fastened around the neck of the corpse, which was lifted up to the surface with relative ease. The small hole was quickly filled in and the corpse bundled away. Canvas would be put down around the grave so that any stray earth could easily be returned, and the grave would look none the different. Their task was made infinitely easier by the large mass burial sites for the poor. Usually just a few inches of soil had to be removed before the cheap, flimsy coffins were revealed, and easily robbed.

Another method was to gain employment as a grave digger, and after the funeral the resurrectionists (as they were also called) would open the coffin and put the body in a sack. Being done six feet below ground, this was very discreet, and as the grave was filled the sack would steadily rise up, to just a few inches below the surface where it would be retrieved under the security of the night. In many cases, the undertakers, and even the sextons would co-operate with the men, receiving a pleasant bonus to their poor wages.

The lack of mortuaries made the body-snatchers' task much easier, as one case in Manchester reflects. The dead were often placed in a spare room in a pub or barn for storage until the funeral. In 1831, the body of a drowned woman was nearly stolen from the Gaythorn Tavern in Manchester, but the plan was foiled just in time.

Another method was brought to the attention of a group of Irish harvestmen in Stockport. One of their fellow workers suffered a rather nasty accident whilst working, and was immediately conveyed to Stockport Infirmary. Unfortunately his injuries were so severe that he passed away, and his friends asked if they could carry the coffin themselves to his place of rest. This they did in a solemn ceremony, but when they first lifted the coffin, they all commented upon how heavy it was. Not wanting to make a fuss, they began walking with the coffin to the churchyard. However, they soon noticed that a large quantity of sand was trickling out from one of the corners, and became suspicious. Still they did not like to interfere with their friend's corpse, and continued walking. Eventually, the coffin had become noticeably lighter in weight, and a long line of sand lay behind them, leading all the way back to the Infirmary. They could conceal their fears no longer, and promptly put the box down, and began to open it. Inside they found no more than grains of sand, their friend's body having fell victim to the knife of the anatomist.

As the "easy money" of the resurrectionists' work attracted more to the grisly career, the general public became outraged, and began to think of methods to stop their nearest and dearests' grave being disturbed. Many large families were able to keep graveside vigils for up to four weeks, after which the body would generally have decomposed to such an extent that it would be of no use to the surgeons.

Opposite: Bodysnatchers at work

Smaller families would place stones and sticks on the new grave, and check if they had been disturbed the next day. This did not stop the body-snatchers though, because they just replaced the items when they had finished! Local gangs were formed to look after newly dug graves, and guard dogs were often used at the entrance to the cemeteries. In Cheadle, Cheshire, locals loaded bundles of sticks and straw onto the hearse, and then buried them in layers with the coffin to foil the body-snatchers.

The burial grounds themselves eventually became more secure, with huge vaults being erected, slabs being laid over graves and iron grills being cemented over the plots. You can still see such constructions in nearly every graveyard in the country.

Such precautions would have been wise in the case of a Stockport man, Henry Walkden, whose aunt passed away on October 22nd, 1791. She was buried in a local churchyard, although it isn't clear which one, but the family seemed to become suspicious of some interference because the coffin was exhumed a month later. Their suspicions were justified because the body had indeed gone- Henry Walkden immediately accused a friend of his, a Dr. C____. in a letter to his son, and summed up this act by saying "It is strange indeed that the bodies of our deceased relatives cannot lie quietly in their graves without being taken out from thence and anatomized by the hands of barbarous cannibles." This anger was understandable from friends and relatives, and often resulted in violent physical attacks upon known body-snatchers.

Bearing in mind the risks they took, the resurrectionists were understandably paid well by the rich surgeons and schools they worked for. It is said that they could earn up to twenty five times the normal man's weekly wage! This was generally spent on beer (considering the gruesome nature of the work, the consumption of alcohol afterwards was greatly appreciated by the men.)

As mentioned earlier, Cheadle was particularly troubled by body-snatchers, the most well-known being Bob Hunt and a Mr. Downes. Bob Hunt was known as a "stockjobber", having been the last man to be put in the village stocks. Mr. Downes was locally renowned for being a successful prize-fighter, and a tale is told of how he sold his own body to a doctor for five pounds (a princely sum in those days!). His body was to be delivered as soon as he died, but the poor doctor lost the deal when he died first, leaving Mr. Downes five pounds richer, and able to look forward to a pleasant spot in a Wilmslow churchyard!

These two men found rich pickings around Cheshire, and were able to sell the corpses to the medical schools in Manchester, having their resurrectionists' rendezvous in the Railway King's public house.

Following the various murders committed in the quest for fresher corpses eg. Burke and Hare (and a man named Hayes who was murdered in Cheadle), the Anatomy Act was rushed through parliament, but the exact details of it were more than a little suspect. Instead of the bodies of murderers being "donated" any body that remained unclaimed after death (i.e. paupers in the workhouse) were permitted to be sold to the anatomists. Ruth Richardson in her book "Death, Dissection and the Destitute", sums up the Anatomy Act perfectly in her statement "What had for generations been a feared and hated punishment for murder became one for poverty." The Anatomy Act is still in force today, but luckily voluntary donations to medical science have made it redundant.

Bibliography

Andrews, William (ed.) "Bygone Cheshire" 1895.

Armand, Muriel. "Ghosts of Cheshire". Countywise Ltd.

Axon, W.E.A. "Cheshire Gleanings". 1884.

Atkinson, Kate."Cage Chronicle"

Beck, Joan. "Tudor Cheshire" Cheshire Community Council. 1969.

Board, Janet and Colin. "Modern Mysteries of Britain" Grafton Books. 1987.

Chambers, Aidan. "Haunted Houses" Pan Books. 1989.

Coward. T.A. "Picturesque Cheshire". 1903.

Coward. T.A. "Cheshire". Methuen and Co. Ltd. 1932.

Fairclough, Charles. "Chester Ghosts and Poltergeists".

Heginbotham, Henry. "Stockport, Ancient and Modern".

Hole, Christina. "Traditions and Customs of Cheshire". 1937.

Ingham, Alfred. "Cheshire, Its Traditions and History" 1920.

Middleton, Thomas. "Legends of Longdendale". 1907.

Mills, Martin. "Supernatural Stockport". Sigma Leisure. 1991.

Moss, Fletcher. "Folklore – Old Customs and Tales of my Neighbours". 1898.

Rae-Ellis, Vivienne. "True Ghost Stories of our own Time". Faber and Faber Ltd. 1990.

Readers' Digest. "Folklore, Myths and Legends of Britain", Readers' Digest Association Ltd. 1977.

Richardson, Ruth. "Death, Dissection and the Destitute", Routledge, Kegan Paul. 1987.

Rickman, Philip. "Mysterious Cheshire" Dalesman Publishing Company Ltd.

Travis, Peter. "In Search of the Supernatural". Wolfe Publishing Ltd. 1975.

We publish guides to individual towns, plus books on walking and cycling in the great outdoors throughout England and Wales.
This is a recent selection:

Local Guidebooks

CHESHIRE: its magic and mystery – Doug Pickford *(£6.95)*

STAFFORDSHIRE: its magic and mystery – Doug Pickford *(£6.95)*

PORTRAIT OF MACCLESFIELD – Doug Pickford *(£6.95)*

PORTRAIT OF MANCHESTER – John Creighton *(£6.95)*

PORTRAIT OF STOCKPORT – John Creighton *(£6.95)*

PORTRAIT OF WARRINGTON – Jen Darling *(£6.95)*

MACCLESFIELD: SO WELL REMEMBERED – Doug Pickford *(£7.95)*

MACCLESFIELD: THOSE WERE THE DAYS – Doug Pickford *(£7.95)*

MAGIC, MYTH AND MEMORIES: The Peak District – Doug Pickford *(£7.95)*

MYTHS AND LEGENDS: East Cheshire and the Moorlands – Doug Pickford *(£7.95)*

SUPERNATURAL STOCKPORT – Martin Mills *(£5.95)*

SHADOWS: a northern investigation of the unknown – Steve Cliffe *(£7.95)*

Sport . . .

RED FEVER:
from Rochdale to Rio as 'United' supporters – Steve Donoghue *(£7.95)*

UNITED WE STOOD:
the unofficial history of the Ferguson years – Richard Kurt *(£6.95)*

MANCHESTER CITY:
Moments to Remember – John Creighton *(£9.95)*

Country Walking . . .

FIFTY CLASSIC WALKS IN THE PENNINES – Terry Marsh *(£8.95)*

RAMBLES IN NORTH WALES – Roger Redfern

HERITAGE WALKS IN THE PEAK DISTRICT – Clive Price

EAST CHESHIRE WALKS – Graham Beech

WEST CHESHIRE WALKS – Jen Darling

WEST PENNINE WALKS – Mike Cresswell

RAMBLES AROUND MANCHESTER – Mike Cresswell

WELSH WALKS: Dolgellau /Cambrian Coast – L. Main & M. Perrott *(£5.95)*

WELSH WALKS: Aberystwyth & District – L. Main & M. Perrott *(£5.95)*
– all of these books are currently £6.95 each, except where indicated

Cycling . . .

CYCLE UK! The essential guide to leisure cycling – Les Lumsdon *(£9.95)*

OFF-BEAT CYCLING IN THE PEAK DISTRICT – Clive Smith *(£6.95)*

MORE OFF-BEAT CYCLING IN THE PEAK DISTRICT – Clive Smith *(£6.95)*

50 BEST CYCLE RIDES IN CHESHIRE – edited by Graham Beech *(£7.95)*

CYCLING IN THE COTSWOLDS – Stephen Hill *(£6.95)*

CYCLING IN THE CHILTERNS – Henry Tindell *(£7.95)*

CYCLING IN SOUTH WALES – Rosemary Evans *(£7.95)*

CYCLING IN LINCOLNSHIRE – Penny & Bill Howe *(£7.95)*

CYCLING IN STAFFORDSHIRE – Linda Wain *(£7.95)*

Explore the Lake District with Sigma!

CYCLING IN THE LAKE DISTRICT – John Wood *(£7.95)*

LAKELAND ROCKY RAMBLES: Geology beneath your feet – Brian Lynas *(£7.95)*

PUB WALKS IN THE LAKE DISTRICT – Neil Coates *(£6.95)*

LAKELAND WALKING, ON THE LEVEL – Norman Buckley *(£6.95)*

MOSTLY DOWNHILL: LEISURELY WALKS, LAKE DISTRICT – Alan Pears *(£6.95)*

THE THIRLMERE WAY – Tim Cappelli *(£6.95)*

THE FURNESS TRAIL – Tim Cappelli *(£6.95)*

Pub Walks . . .

A fabulous series of 'Pub Walks' books for just about every popular walking area in the UK, all featuring access by public transport

– plus many more entertaing and educational books being regularly added to our list. All of our books are available from your local bookshop. In case of difficulty, or to obtain our complete catalogue, please contact:

**Sigma Leisure, 1 South Oak Lane, Wilmslow, Cheshire SK9 6AR
Phone: 0625 – 531035   Fax: 0625 – 536800**

ACCESS and VISA orders welcome – call our friendly sales staff or use our 24 hour Answerphone service! Most orders are despatched on the day we receive your order – you could be enjoying our books in just a couple of days.